797,885 Books
are available to read at

www.ForgottenBooks.com

Forgotten Books' App
Available for mobile, tablet & eReader

ISBN 978-1-332-42799-4
PIBN 10425599

This book is a reproduction of an important historical work. Forgotten Books uses state-of-the-art technology to digitally reconstruct the work, preserving the original format whilst repairing imperfections present in the aged copy. In rare cases, an imperfection in the original, such as a blemish or missing page, may be replicated in our edition. We do, however, repair the vast majority of imperfections successfully; any imperfections that remain are intentionally left to preserve the state of such historical works.

Forgotten Books is a registered trademark of FB &c Ltd.
Copyright © 2015 FB &c Ltd.
FB &c Ltd, Dalton House, 60 Windsor Avenue, London, SW19 2RR.
Company number 08720141. Registered in England and Wales.

For support please visit www.forgottenbooks.com

1 MONTH OF
FREE
READING

at
www.ForgottenBooks.com

By purchasing this book you are eligible for one month membership to ForgottenBooks.com, giving you unlimited access to our entire collection of over 700,000 titles via our web site and mobile apps.

To claim your free month visit:
www.forgottenbooks.com/free425599

* Offer is valid for 45 days from date of purchase. Terms and conditions apply.

Similar Books Are Available from
www.forgottenbooks.com

Beautiful Joe
An Autobiography, by Marshall Saunders

Theodore Roosevelt, an Autobiography
by Theodore Roosevelt

Napoleon
A Biographical Study, by Max Lenz

Up from Slavery
An Autobiography, by Booker T. Washington

Gotama Buddha
A Biography, Based on the Canonical Books of the Theravādin, by Kenneth J. Saunders

Plato's Biography of Socrates
by A. E. Taylor

Cicero
A Biography, by Torsten Petersson

Madam Guyon
An Autobiography, by Jeanne Marie Bouvier De La Motte Guyon

The Writings of Thomas Jefferson
by Thomas Jefferson

Thomas Skinner, M.D.
A Biographical Sketch, by John H. Clarke

Saint Thomas Aquinas of the Order of Preachers (1225-1274)
A Biographical Study of the Angelic Doctor, by Placid Conway

Recollections of the Rev. John Johnson and His Home
An Autobiography, by Susannah Johnson

Biographical Sketches in Cornwall, Vol. 1 of 3
by R. Polwhele

Autobiography of John Francis Hylan, Mayor of New York
by John Francis Hylan

The Autobiography of Benjamin Franklin
The Unmutilated and Correct Version, by Benjamin Franklin

James Mill
A Biography, by Alexander Bain

George Washington
An Historical Biography, by Horace E. Scudder

Florence Nightingale
A Biography, by Irene Cooper Willis

Marse Henry
An Autobiography, by Henry Watterson

Autobiography and Poems
by Charlotte E. Linden

UNIV. OF
CALIFORNIA

H.M. THE QUEEN OF BULGARIA.

WAR AND WOMEN

FROM EXPERIENCE IN THE BALKANS AND ELSEWHERE

BY

MRS. ST. CLAIR STOBART

FOUNDER OF THE WOMEN'S CONVOY CORPS

WITH A PREFACE BY
VISCOUNT ESHER, G.C.B.

LONDON
G. BELL & SONS LTD.
1913

WAR AND WOMEN

FROM EXPERIENCE IN THE BALKANS AND ELSEWHERE

BY

Mrs. ST. CLAIR STOBART
FOUNDER OF THE WOMEN'S CONVOY CORPS

WITH A PREFACE BY
VISCOUNT ESHER, G.C.B.

LONDON
G. BELL & SONS LTD.
1913

DR46
S8

DEDICATED

TO

THE QUEEN OF BULGARIA

BY HER MAJESTY'S GRACIOUS PERMISSION

PREFATORY NOTE

By VISCOUNT ESHER, G.C.B.

I HAVE been asked to write a few introductory words to this book.

As President of the County of London Territorial Association I became acquainted with Mrs. St. Clair Stobart and her work. We have differed much in opinion, but we have worked well together for the interests of the Territorial Force. Like her, I have resigned my connection with the British Red Cross Society, not being satisfied that the organization, plan and sphere of operations of the society, although philanthropic, are framed with a sole view to the welfare of our country.

When Mrs. St. Clair Stobart told me that she was going to the Balkans with the Convoy Corps, I reminded her of my publicly stated objections to sending assistance to foreign armies engaged in war, on the ground that any help whatever (however humane the motive) is a breach of neutrality and is tantamount to taking part in the war. This record of the

Convoy Corps' achievements in the Balkans proves how effectively a body of well-meaning, philanthropic and earnest folk can assist combatants, patching up wounded to go and kill and maim their opponents, thus breaking the law of neutrality as completely as though they supplied arms, or cash, or munitions of war, or even volunteers, in a cause which is not the cause of our land and people.

Mrs. St. Clair Stobart has, however, done this great service. She has proved by experience and example what women can achieve in war, and although I am not prepared to accept all her inferences and assent to all her deductions on the disputed position of women in the social ordinance of civilized states, it is impossible to resist her plea for a reconsideration of the place assigned to them in the scheme of National Defence.

Nursing the sick and wounded in war is clearly women's work. The detailed arrangements, their plan and ordering, are a sphere of activity for women in peace. As matters now stand, nursing schemes are worked out and stereotyped by the military authorities, without advice or suggestion from those who, in war, will have to bear the chief burden. The plea has always been that the hierarchy of the

PREFATORY NOTE

R.A.M.C. know all about war and its requirements, whereas women know nothing. This book disposes of that fallacy. It is doubtful whether any R.A.M.C. officer can claim an experience equal to that of the Convoy Corps and its medical staff. Has full advantage been taken of this experience so dearly purchased by weeks of physical and moral suffering? I should be curious to know.

In Russia and in Japan the Red Cross Society is admirably organized, and its work is far reaching in peace and war. In Great Britain there is no one body or one authority that corresponds to the Red Cross Society in those countries. Here there are, as usual, cross-currents in peace and sure confusion in war. The respective spheres of the British Red Cross Society, the Order of St. John, and the R.A.M.C. are quite undefined, and urgently require definition.

If Mrs. St. Clair Stobart's book succeeds in drawing public attention to the want of sound organization for the relief of the sick and wounded in the schemes of imperial offence and defence, it will have achieved the object with which I hope it was planned and written.

ESHER.

PROEM

WHEN it was first suggested to me—on my return from the Balkans—that I should write a book describing my experiences during the war, I was taken by surprise. "Oh no! certainly not," I answered. "Why! it would be all about myself." It had, besides, never occurred to me that anything had been accomplished worthy of being "written about." I had done what I set out to do, and there was an end of it I thought. I had wished to give a practical demonstration of the fact that women are capable of taking an independent and serviceable share in National Defence. That demonstration was successful, and thereafter it was *Nunc Dimittis* as far as I was concerned.

But then it was borne in upon me, that unless this demonstration was a demonstration *to the Public* its significance as an object lesson would be lost. It was my duty, I was told, to place on record the experiences of this little company of women, who had, after opposition from the

Home authorities, performed on their own, amidst some difficulties, in a foreign country, work which has not before been done exclusively by women—within the area of war.

I then realized that the object which I have at heart—the inclusion of women as practical and living factors in the Territorial Service—might be adversely affected by my silence. It is useless to toy with Ideas. Ideas, if they are worth anything, must be hammered in. It was horrible for me that there was nobody *else* to do this particular bit of hammering, but as it had to be done I yielded. I am not a writer of books, and I dislike publicity. To be thus compelled to write in book form, and in the first person singular, was a double nightmare. I confess I would almost rather have gone through my war experiences again than have written about them.

But now it is done, and I am only anxious that those who may read the story shall understand that it has not been written under the belief that we accomplished during our Balkan expedition anything wonderful There was nothing wonderful about it The book has been written solely with a view to showing that women can be of independent service in National Defence.

The experiences I have gained in the Balkans

have taught me many things. As a result, I am convinced that if women are to become *efficient* members of a National Service, and are to be allowed to give to the nation's defences *of their very best*, they must no longer be played with, as at present, by the British Red Cross Society's scheme of Voluntary Aid Detachments. They must be trained and adopted wholeheartedly by the Territorial Army. Women must no longer be regarded as apocryphal numbers, but as worthy to be included in the inspired text of the national religion of Patriotism.

As a protest in this direction, I have resigned my membership of the County Committee, and also of the Executive Council of the County of London branch, of the British Red Cross Society, because I feel that the telescopes of this society are, as concerns the work of women, directed to the *Past* rather than to the *Future*, and there is no hope that under the ægis of this organization anything practical will result.

From the moment when the B.R.C.S. inaugurated, under the War Office, its system of V.A.D.'s, I have, in conducting the " Women's Convoy Corps," worked loyally with the former Society in the hope that through them my ultimate aim of obtaining for women an adequate training would be fulfilled. I am now, however, convinced that the B.R.C.S. is not the appropriate medium for providing the country with an imperially and *practically* trained body of women. That being my belief, I have felt it necessary to resign, not only from the B.R.C. Society's committees, but also from the *Women's Convoy Corps*, of which I was the founder, and the organizing commandant. For the Corps has always been—from the time of the inception of the V.A.D. scheme—intimately associated with the Red Cross Society. And rather than ask the Corps to sacrifice this official respectability and come out into the wilderness with me—I have resigned and become a free lance.

It is not without sorrow that I relinquish the fellowship of an organization which had become an intimate portion of my life, and dissociate myself from Red Cross work. But paper protests are valueless. And though the B.R.C.S. is a large and influential body, and is not likely to be affected by my secession, I believe that no genuine pro*test*-ant ever protests quite in vain.

Upon the two subjects with which the book deals—" War and Women," I have probably spoken more firmly than will be commendable to many. But for anybody who has passed the jelly-fish stage of existence it would have been impossible to encounter war in the Balkans, and women there and elsewhere, as I encountered them, without deriving from these experiences strong impressions—one way or another.

I condemn war—and therefore militarists will be offended. And I vindicate women, and anti-feminists will perhaps be shocked. But condemnation and vindication are both alike based, not upon book-derived theories, but upon practical observation. I can therefore offer no apology for presenting untainted evidence.

But both militarists and anti-feminists will probably, in chorus, accuse me of inconsistency. How, they will demand, is it possible logically to condemn war as a barbarism, and yet in one and the same breath to plead that women should participate in war? But the inconsistency is on the part of the governments of Europe. These spend millions annually in providing materials for the mutual destruction of each other's armies, and then expend further millions in providing hospitals, surgeons, and Red Cross paraphernalia for the restoration to life of those same armies.

If these governments have made up their minds that it is virtuous to *kill* their enemies —in accordance with the Mohammedan rather than the Christian faith—it would be more consistent if they abolished Red Cross work. But no man in Europe has the courage of this conviction. In the meantime, so long as the honour of the *men* of a nation is involved in *taking* life, so long must the honour of *women* be concerned in the attempt to *save* life. From this there is no logical escape. And for this reason, Women and War—Beauty and the Beast—must make their grim alliance.

M. A. STOBART.

LIST OF ILLUSTRATIONS

H.M. THE QUEEN OF BULGARIA	*Frontispiece*
	FACING PAGE
SERVIAN PEASANTRY IN BELGRADE	24
A MOSQUE IN SOFIA	34
MILITARY TRAINS WITH BULGARIAN SOLDIERS ON THEIR WAY TO THE FRONT	42
BULLOCK WAGGON IN JAMBOLI	50
STREET IN SOFIA, SHOWING (AT THE END OF THE STREET) ONE ENTRANCE TO THE ROYAL PALACE	58
THE PRINCESSES EUDOXIE AND NADEZDA OF BULGARIA	68
PIETRO WITH MY BULLOCK WAGGON	76
WOMEN'S CONVOY CORPS ON TREK	78
TURKISH AMMUNITION CARTS CAPTURED BY THE BULGARIANS AT THE FRONTIER VILLAGE OF DERVENT	80
WOMEN'S CONVOY CORPS CROSSING THE BULGARIAN-TURKISH FRONTIER	82
A THRACIAN WELL, WITH BULGARIAN PEASANTS	84
BULGARIAN PEASANTS SPINNING AND REELING YARN	86
MY OX, JUST AFTER HE HAS EATEN MY BED	88
CONVOY CORPS ON TREK—BREAKFAST OUTSPAN	88
CONVOY CORPS ON TREK—A MIDDAY HALT	92

LIST OF ILLUSTRATIONS

	FACING PAGE
A Devastated Village between Jamboli and Kirk-Kilisse .	94
Kirk-Kilisse from the South .	100
Women's Convoy Corps Hospital—Houses Left and Right of Flags	106
One of the Wards, Women's Convoy Corps Hospital	112
Some of the Women's Convoy Corps Hospital Staff	114
Group of some Convalescents, Doctors, Nurses, Orderlies, Interpreters .	124
Post Office in Kirk-Kilisse .	136
The Bishop of Stara Zagora, an Attendant Priest, and one of our English Interpreters	144
Hospital Kitchen Staff	150
Some of the 140 guns at Kirk-Kilisse captured by the Bulgarians .	160
Group of Convalescent Patients going Home .	168
Interpreter persuading Peasant that Five Francs in the Pocket is worth more than a Turkey-cock on the Green	182
A Satisfactory Bargain over Turkey	186
Good-bye to Kirk-Kilisse	198
Field Hospital near Adrianople	202
In the Trenches near Adrianople	204

WAR AND WOMEN

CHAPTER I

For the first time in history a company composed exclusively of women has had the experience of going to the front in a campaign, and of improvizing and administering, in a foreign country, a hospital for sick and wounded soldiers.

The Women's Convoy Corps was invited by Queen Eleonora, by the Bulgarian Red Cross Society, and by the Bulgarian Medical Military authorities, to render assistance during the war of the Balkan States against the Turks. The contingent which went out in response was self-contained as to doctors, nurses, cooks, etc., and numbered, including myself as organizer and administrator, sixteen.

I propose in the following pages to describe the experiences with which we met during our ten weeks in Bulgaria, and also to discuss the general subject of "Women in warfare," and to attempt to answer the question, "*Ought* women to take a *practical* share in National Defence, and to be included as an integral portion of the Territorial Service?"

Now, this innocent-looking word "ought" is the most misleading word in the dictionary. For it assumes a plain and pious issue between something that is comfortably right and something else that is definitely wrong, whereas public opinion—the sole arbiter of standards of right and wrong—never recognizes that a thing is *right* till it has been shown to be *expedient*. And this makes all the difference, for it means that if you really want to convince the public that a thing is right and that it *ought* to be done, you must prove to the public that the thing will be *expedient* for the public—that it will not, that is, injure more public interests than it will serve.

But expediency cannot be proved by either of the two arch-humbugs which are usually trotted out to cajole the unwary. Expediency cannot be proved by either *argument* or *figures*.

Argument can prove that black is white (black grown shabby gets grey, white grown dirty gets grey, and things that are equal to the same thing are equal to one another, Q.E.D.).

And *figures* can prove—on properly manipulated balance sheets—that income and expenditure have hit it off to the very farthing—a proposition which is for most of us an obvious absurdity.

But "argument makes the mob mistrustful" and figures are for the multitude "figures of speech" only. The arts and wiles of argument and of figures combined are powerless to persuade that conservative old entity "Public Opinion" that some new course of action will be for his interest, *until this has been proved by "practical demonstration."*

Florence Nightingale might, for instance, have argued with the eloquence of Demosthenes that it was *right* for a woman to nurse the sick and wounded, and that she *ought* to be allowed to face the horrors of the Crimean War for that purpose. She would never have got there. She, however showed, the genius of the true reformer. She *demonstrated by practical methods* her capacity for alleviating suffering, and by *conduct*, not words, proved the expediency for all concerned of allowing women to do work for which nature has specially fitted them. "Between vague wavering capability and fixed indubitable performance," as Carlyle puts it, "what a difference!"

And now the Women's Convoy Corps have given a *practical demonstration* of the capacity of women to be of independent service in warfare. It is hoped, therefore, that this account of their work may help to prove the *expediency* of allowing women not only to work in hospitals of war, but to take a responsible position in the Territorial Service of the country.

CHAPTER II

THE origin of the Convoy Corps was as follows: I had been living for some years on the African veldt—in the Transvaal—where one was face to face with real things, big things, things of life and death. No one had time out there to *write* about things or to *talk* about things,—one had to *do* things. But when I came back to London, I found everybody very busy writing, and very busy talking, about two great dangers which were at that moment supposed to be threatening England.

The first was invasion of this country by Germany. This was expected every morning at breakfast-time with the arrival of the *Daily Mail*, and judging by the Press generally, and by the conversations at clubs, street-corners, and dinner-tables, the population was in a real state of panic. But I was surprised to find that the golf-courses, bridge-tables and other familiar centres for the unemployable were no less crowded than usual with men who talked tearfully of the rotten state of the Territorial Army, but were themselves doing nothing for its salvation, and with men and women who deplored the unpreparedness of England for the landing of the Germans, but seemed unanimously to think it was somebody else's job to be prepared.

The other danger with which I found England confronted, was the possibility of the granting of the parliamentary franchise to women. I had not at that time studied the question, but I was struck with the quaint way in which women were ignoring the one *proof* of *expediency* which was to hand.

Women refused to see that the best way of *proving* to Public Opinion their power of judgment in political matters concerned with the *larger* and imperial parliament, was to give a *practical demonstration* of their political judgment as elected members of the *lesser* parliaments (the county and municipal councils).

But women, I found, took an interest in municipal elections precisely in inverse ratio to their interest in "Votes for Women." In burlesque fashion, this only available *practical demonstration* of women's political capacity, was being exploited by the *anti*-suffragists, who argued that though women were unfitted to select others—even though these others were men—to do work, in the larger parliament, for which there is little individual responsibility—they *are* fitted to be themselves selected to perform, in the lesser parliaments, work for which there is, in the absence of an autocratic cabinet, *much* individual responsibility. A Gilbertian climax was presently reached. Believing that municipal work is women's work, believing further that "Conviction is worthless till it is converted into Conduct," I accepted an invitation, in March 1913, to stand for Westminster in the forlorn cause of Progressivism for election to the London County Council.

I then found that the *suffrage* societies were all too busy "getting the parliamentary vote" to be able to assist in securing the return of one of the few women who were standing as L.C.C. candidates, whilst the *anti*-suffrage societies, which are concerned with showing that municipal work *is* the one and only legitimate outlet for women's *political* activities, would not assist my candidature because, forsooth, I was—though not a militant suffragist—a believer in the *political* enfranchisement of women!

But these two dangers—invasion by Germany and invasion by Women,—the Scylla and Charybdis upon which it was feared the British Empire might at any moment founder—had neither of them, at the time of my return to London from the Transvaal, been investigated by me. Embued, however, as I was, with the practical philosophy of the veldt, I was at once struck by the juxtaposition in time and space of these two problems. The coincidence seemed, as far as women were concerned, full of interest and significance.

For, if it were, on the one hand, true, that the country was momentarily liable to invasion by a powerful enemy, and that our defence was, as represented, totally inadequate, then it seemed obvious that the help of women might usefully be employed in National Defence. Whilst as concerning the right of women to the parliamentary franchise, how, I argued, could women *prove* that they were capable of taking a share in the work of national and imperial parliaments, unless and until they had shown their capacity for taking an *interest* in national and imperial affairs?

So long as women's interests were purely personal and parochial, so long must their influence remain personal and parochial. And how better could they show their interest in national and imperial affairs than by taking a share in *National Defence?* For if women desired to share in the *government* of the country, it seemed plain to me that they must share in the responsibility of *defending* the country. And—here is the bedrock cause of the foundation of the Women's Convoy Corps —the only way of showing that they are capable of taking a real share in National Defence is to *prove* it—by *practical demonstration.*

This task—of demonstration—seemed well worth while, since two birds of public danger would be hit by one stone. I felt convinced that there must be some form of service in which I myself, for instance, could be of use in national emergency, and what I could do, could also—so I argued to myself—be done by thousands of other women. I therefore set to work neither to write nor to talk, but to *do.*

My first task was to discover whether there was anywhere within the Territorial organization, a gap wherein the services of women could usefully be employed. I found my gap in that sphere of operations which occurs between the field and the base hospitals. For, according to the usual routine, the wounded receive first-aid treatment and are removed from the battlefield to the field hospital by the Royal Army Medical Corps, and so far all is well. But the R.A.M.C. are a mobile force and have to move on to other battles with the troops. From the moment, therefore, that the wounded have been first-aided and deposited in the field hospital, they are left to the tender mercies of voluntary orderlies or stray benefactors to take charge of them during their convoy to the evacuation hospitals along the lines of communication, or to the base hospitals, which may be at a distance of many days' journey by road or rail. Precisely during the precious first hours, or it may be days, when most care is needed, least is procurable, and experience recently gained during the war in the Balkans more than confirms this earlier belief, that in every branch of work that occurs within this zone of operations, the activities of women could usefully be employed.

With a view, therefore, to training women to be of general service in all forms of work occurring *between the field hospital and the base,* the Women's Convoy Corps was inaugurated. I was fortunate enough to secure the co-operation of Major Langford Lloyd, D.S.O., who was at that time head of the R.A.M.C. School of

Instruction in London. With the help derived from his practical knowledge of the requirements, a three years' course of training was instituted, and the following subjects were included in the curriculum :—

> First Aid, Nursing, Cooking (plain, convalescent and camp), Laundry, Housewifery, Signalling (Morse and Semaphore), Driving (horse and motor), Riding, Cycling, Map-reading and making.
>
> Life-saving (in water), Stretcher and Ambulance work, Waggon drill, Fire drill, Improvization work in field and in hospitals, etc.
>
> An annual Camp.

In camp the women live in tents, which they pitch and strike themselves. They dig their own camp-fire trenches, construct their own camp-kitchen, and cook their own food in the open, whatever the weather may be. They perform all their own quartermastering and stewards' work, sleep on straw mattresses, in unboarded tents, and, without the aid of male hewers of wood and drawers of water, undergo a general training in improvization, discipline and self-reliance, and learn, generally speaking, to approximate as nearly as possible to conditions likely to obtain in time of war.

Of these subjects some, as will be seen, have

a *direct* educational value for the object in view, whilst others have for their main object training in resourcefulness, self-sacrifice, endurance, discipline,—the evolution, in short, of a body of imperially-trained women ready to turn their hands to any work which the nation may in emergency require of them.

But, it will be suggested, "is not *hospital nursing* given a much too insignificant place in this scheme of work? Surely *nursing* should be the first and foremost, if not the sole, object of training? It is within the *hospitals* that woman's work must lie." This is the view apparently held by the B.R.C. authorities and the War Office, who have—since the inauguration of the Convoy Corps—organized a scheme of V.A.D.'s composed respectively of women and of men, to look after the home defences of the sick and wounded. But I contend—and my experience in the Balkan War confirms me in my belief—that it is not within the organized and fully equipped base hospitals that the help of volunteers, men or women, is, in time of war, required. There exists already in this country a magnificent staff of fully trained nurses who are competent to deal in hospitals with ward work—from which amateurs and volunteers are better excluded.

It takes a trained nurse three years of continuous training and drudgery within the walls of a hospital, to learn the work and discipline of the wards, and it is absurd to imagine that a few lectures on first-aid and home nursing, even supplemented by an occasional odd day or two, or even a few weeks, in the out-patients' department or the wards of a friendly hospital, is going to qualify a woman who is not making nursing *her work in life* to understand all the intricacies and to deal with the diseases and conditions incidental to ward work.

The distinction between professional and amateur is probably in no profession more marked or of more importance than in that of nursing, and it seemed to me for every reason desirable that the sphere of the *professional* nurse should be clearly differentiated from that of the *volunteer* nurse. The latter should be regarded not so much as a nurse, as a *first-aider*, to give first aid *in every department of work occurring between the field hospital and the base.* The distinction between trained nurse and volunteer first-aider should be complete both as to work and uniform. It was, to my mind, grotesque that women, after attending half a dozen lectures on first-aid and home nursing, should be allowed, as under the régime of the B.R.C.S. and the War Office, to wear a *nurse's* uniform and regard themselves as fully competent members of a V.A.D., qualified to take their places in a scheme of National Defence.

It is not within the wards of base hospitals, but in improvization and in the rough and ready emergency work required in *getting the wounded to the base hospitals*, that the help of those who cannot give their whole life to the work of nursing is required. It was with a view to training women for this object, that subjects extraneous to nursing, such as ambulance-waggon-driving, riding, cooking, washing, map-reading, etc., were included in the curriculum of the Women's Convoy Corps.

CHAPTER III

THIS training had been satisfactorily in progress during four years, and afforded every reason for belief that women *trained* and *disciplined* could take a responsible share in warfare without the need of Gibeonites of the male sex, who ought all, if able-bodied, to be in the *fighting* line. But no opportunity of putting the training to a practical test had, up to the autumn of 1912, occurred, and I was obliged to content myself with the knowledge that an imperially-minded body of women was being trained for any national emergency which might arise, and that this training was also of *present* value in that it taught women to be of greater service in their own homes in *domestic* emergency in time of *peace*, as well as of potential value in *national* emergency in time of *war*.

But in October of 1912 the Balkan war-cloud burst. Bulgaria, Servia, Greece, and Montenegro declared war against their traditional enemy, the Turk. The newspapers reported that thousands of wounded were daily being poured into hospitals which were overcrowded and understaffed, and it was obvious that the arrangements for nursing the sick and wounded were generally inadequate. The expediency of admitting women as *nurses* in the *wards* of hospitals of war had already been proved. Here, it seemed, was an opportunity of proving the expediency of *extending* the sphere of operations of women's work in war. I realized that, at all costs, advantage must be taken of an occasion unique for the purpose of testing character, by the opportunities it would probably afford of difficulties and hardships to be encountered and overcome. I heard that the B.R.C.S. was dispatching units to nurse the sick and wounded, and I at once applied, for myself and for specially selected members of the Convoy Corps, to be included amongst the first volunteers to be sent to the front.

Every member of the Convoy Corps is also a member of a V.A.D. registered with the B.R.C.S. at the War Office, the work and value of the training of the Corps was well known and appreciated by the B.R.C.S. as well as by the W.O., and as only those members were offered for service who possessed special qualifications, either as trained nurses or for length of service in the corps, I had every hope that my offer would be accepted.

My feelings, therefore, can be imagined when the fiat went forth that the B.R.C.S. intended to send units consisting of *men only* to nurse the sick and wounded! Men of whom some—as was eventually revealed—knew more about the rules of football than of hospital work. There was, it was said, "no work fitted for women in the Balkans." Now I ought, doubtless, meekly to have acquiesced in this decision of the supreme authorities. I *was* meek for half a day, and then I realized that many fully trained women nurses outside the Corps, even better qualified than some of us, were also offering their services and were being refused *because they were women*, and I felt that the whole cause of women's work in war and national defence was in danger of being retrograded by this decision of the B.R.C.S. For women were now being kept back even from that sphere of work which Florence Nightingale had, as we imagined, conquered for women once and for ever. I determined, therefore, to go out to the Balkans and see for myself whether there was, indeed, no work "fitted for women," or whether, as I suspected, the truth was that the B.R.C.S. *imagined* there were no women fitted for the work. I knew better. I knew that there were plenty of women admirably fitted for the nursing of sick and wounded, *whatever the conditions might be.* I believed that any work for which women were fitted was work fitted for women, and I made up my mind to judge for myself *upon the spot* as to whether the conditions in the Balkans were prohibitive, or whether there was not, indeed, work in which *trained and disciplined women* could well in such a crisis be of use. If, after investigation of all the circumstances, I should find that the work was unsuitable for women —an unlikely contingency where nursing was concerned—no harm would have been done, but I should myself presumably gain some experiences of conditions in hospitals of war. If, on the other hand, I should find, as I fully expected, that the services of *trained and disciplined* women were urgently needed, I could cable to the members of the Corps, who had already been selected, to join me wherever our work should be required.

The selection of candidates for this service necessarily caused some heartburnings, for in addition to technical qualifications, length of service in the Corps, knowledge of French and German, age (no one under twenty-eight was eligible), and stability—both psychical and physiological—had to be taken into account. Doctors (women) from outside the Corps had also to be selected, for though no definite idea could be formed as to what work would be likely to be required, I formed a notion in my own mind as to the work I wished to do. I selected women rather than men doctors, for the purpose of fully demonstrating my argument that women are capable of undertaking *all* work in connection with the sick and wounded in warfare. Had I waived this principle as regards the medical staff I ran the risk of being told, if the experiment should succeed, or equally if it should fail, " Ah, yes! but then, you see, you had *male* doctors with you!"

But provisory arrangements were quickly made, and I found myself, after a preparation of two days, entrained on the Orient Express, en route via Paris, Vienna and Buda Pesth for Belgrade—the capital of Servia.

CHAPTER IV

BELGRADE was reached after forty-eight hours of uneventful travel. It was here that I gained my first experience of war conditions, and as I walked through ward after ward of the first hospital I visited, I understood the value of a "first impression."

The soldiers objected to open windows, the rooms were small, there was no ventilation, and the evil odours of gangrenous wounds and repulsive smelling disinfectants—the sight of room after room, crammed to every available inch of space with men who had been *made* after a design that was godlike, but were now mutilated out of recognition of any design—that first impression of the results of war had for me the significance of a revelation.

I had left England believing with most people that though war is in some ways undoubtedly an evil, it *may*, on the other hand, as contended, "evoke qualities of heroism which would otherwise lie dormant," and that it might thus possibly have a place in the universal scheme. But as I looked at those blood-smeared bodies—those mangled human remnants, suffering tortures that had been inflicted *by* man *upon* man, and was conscious that, in hundreds of hospitals throughout the Balkans, the same ghastly tragedy was at that moment being presented—I knew that sanction for such carnage could only come from sophists whose vision of life is limited to the material. "The manhood that has been in war must," says Emerson placidly, "be transferred to the cause of peace before war can lose its charm and peace be venerable to men." But if the cause of peace is able, in this twentieth century, to offer no greater opportunities for the exercise of manhood and heroic qualities than were expended in producing suffering like this, then, I felt, life itself has no significance, and the motto that should be inscribed for each new-born child over the portals of its entrance to this world should be, *not* "Enter ye into the life everlasting," *but* "Abandon hope all ye that enter here." Thenceforth I regarded the suffering in the Balkan hospitals as a litany in which I too must join—a litany to the God of Peace—a supplication for the enlightenment of Europe.

In this big military hospital which I first visited, there were 600 wounded soldiers, 7 doctors, and 50 untrained volunteer and local women nurses. All the larger houses and every available gymnasium (school), institution or hall in Belgrade had, of course, also been converted into improvized hospitals. Conditions varied in accordance with the available resources and the prevailing personality of the director of the hospital. But everywhere the wards were, of necessity, overcrowded, the staff of doctors pitiably undermanned and the nursing almost entirely carried out by volunteer local ladies and peasant women utterly untrained for their grim, gigantic task.

The smell of some of those unventilated wards, overheated with iron stoves, is not easily forgotten. One room in which the odour and the heat were particularly offensive, measured—as I roughly estimated—eighteen feet by fourteen feet, and contained at the moment of my visit 24 people, including 12 patients, doctors, nurses and visitors, and there was not an inch of open window anywhere. One soldier in this room was specially on show. He had been wounded in the left arm, and the bullet was said to have made its exit—after the manner of a conjurer's egg—from his right side. He boasted proudly that he had killed 20 Turks with one bayonet,—presumably not all with one thrust. He presented me with an exploded hand grenade which had been thrown by Kurds and had killed one of his friends. Another soldier in this same room had been hit in the shoulder by a shell—in fourteen places. "The more the merrier" apparently—for he was particularly cheerful and showed me with pride a silver snuff-box which he had looted from a dead Turkish officer. He was in great pain, but he was, he said, trying to get well as quickly as possible so that he might go back and have "another go at the Turks." And yet in many of the rooms—though Turkish *officers* were placed in a room apart—Turkish soldiers and Albanians (Arnots) were lying in the same wards, mixed indiscriminately amongst their Servian enemies.

The dead, too, frequently lay side by side with the living, undivided even by a screen. I noticed a specially fine-looking young Servian peasant, who, without disfiguring bandages or splints, was lying quiet and motionless with closed eyes. He had been shot through the lungs. "He is passing over," said a nurse as I stood and looked at him. "In a few minutes he'll be dead." By the bedside sat an old white-haired man, dressed in the sheepskin coat, baggy breeches and white navushtas of the Servian peasantry. His eyes were riveted on the face of his only son. Suddenly the boy sat up, struggled for breath, gave a last look at his father, and fell back—dead. The old man grasped the unresponsive hand "*Pietro*," he cried—then looked in consternation at the nurse—a Servian lady volunteer. She said nothing, but fetched a candle and, lighting it, placed it at the head of the bed. The father understood and, whilst the last offices were performed, sat in silence—his face hidden in his hands. Then at a word from the nurse he rose, looked for the last time at the beloved face—a sheet was flung over the dead boy, and in silence the old man, without looking back, walked with bent head down the ward and went out—childless.

There was too much to be done for the living, there was no time for sentiment towards the dead or dying. In the next bed, another soldier, about to join his dead comrade, was tossing restlessly, and plucking at the blanket. The nurse, impatient to get on to other work, was trying to make the dying man take paper and pencil in his hand. He petulantly refused. "He won't believe," she said, "that he

SERVIAN PEASANTRY IN BELGRADE.

is dying. We want his name—he has no number." "But I'm *not* dying," he gurgled—"I shall——" But the sentence was never finished—he fell back—he had passed from the reek of battlefields and the fetid smell of hospitals to a happier resthouse—where no number was required.

"Do you write to the relatives?" I asked.

"Oh no!" replied the nurse—a Servian lady of society—"there's no time for things like that,"—and she hurried away to help put back into his bed a man who, though suffering from compound fracture of both legs, was, with others, returning from the surgery, where he had been taken to have his wounds dressed. For, owing to the scarcity of doctors and the fact that there were few, if any, trained nurses, it was customary in some of the improvized hospitals for all the dressings to be done in the surgery; and the patients had to run the risks and endure the pain of being carried, when absolute immobility was essential, by peasant men unused to the work, up and down the stairs and through the long winding corridors, every time the dressings were changed.

But great as was the need for trained nurses at Belgrade, there was no lack of local volunteers, and I felt that Belgrade was not near enough to the active zone of operations for my purpose. I therefore—after visiting as many of the improvized hospitals as the hours of one day would allow, and after also paying a visit to the wife of the British Minister, who was herself working day and night in one of the hospitals—went on to Sofia, the Bulgarian capital.

CHAPTER V

THE train took twenty-four hours, the railway service being of course disorganized and given up to conveying soldiers, guns and military stores to the front, and carrying the wounded to hospitals along the lines of communication. There was no sleeping accommodation or dining car, and any restaurants there might be at wayside stations were always besieged by starving soldiers, and were quite inaccessible. But a lesson in frugality was given by a fellow-traveller—a fine old Servian priest of the Greek Church—Tsched Schljivitsch by name. He was more than contented with occasional slender portions of brown bread and cheese, which he had brought with him, and never seemed to know the need of drinking. He was in great spirits, having just left his wife and thirteen children, and his parish near Nisch, to go to the front—not in his ecclesiastical capacity, but to *fight*. He had enlisted in what was called a free regiment—a regiment, that is, of volunteers. He wore his usual garments, an overcoat over a long black cassock, black breeches, coloured, home-knit stockings, long boots and a black astrachan cap with a small gilt cross in the centre of the front. I asked him in the German language, in which we were conversing, how he reconciled his Christian principles of "loving" his brethren with his eagerness to fight and kill his fellow-men? He promptly dived into his deep pockets and produced a Testament printed in the old Slavish text, and read aloud in triumphant tone, " He who *loves* his brother will *die* for his brother." " My brethren have for centuries," he said, "been killed and tortured by the Turks. I will help to deliver them. I fight," he added, " with *two* weapons—the rifle "—in mock show he extended his arm and took aim—"and with the crucifix," and as he spoke he kissed a crucifix worn on a long chain round his neck, then put it back reverently under his cassock.

" But "—I asked, with sympathetic experience of the inconvenience of skirts when active work is on hand—" how do you manage to fight in that long cassock? Isn't it horribly in the way?"

"Oh no! that's quite simply managed," he

replied. "See here," and in a second he had tucked it all up on both sides through the pocket-slits, leaving his legs quite comfortably free.

But my fine old friend wasn't only a warrior and a priest, he was also a poet, and was carrying in his handbag a whole packet of unbound booklets of poems composed by himself. He had written them specially, he said, to stimulate his fellow-soldiers at the front, and judging by some of those which he translated into German for my benefit, he was better as poet than as priest. For the verses, though they all breathed the fire-and-slaughter spirit of mediæval times, were full of poetry and inspiration. They afforded to me a naive illustration of the fact that my apparently refined and cultured friend was in *reality* representative of a plane of thought which elsewhere in Europe would only have been appropriate in the Middle Ages. Indeed, in these poems the prototype used throughout as the main incentive to heroism, was that old fourteenth-century Servian hero, Stephen Dushan, self-styled "Czar of Macedonia, Monarch of the Serbs, Greeks, and Bulgarians and people of the western coast"!—"The Throttler," as he was surnamed by others—and not inaptly, for he was a prodigal builder of churches, sure sign in those days that he had committed many crimes for which atonement was required.

The subject of one poem which I specially remember, concerned an old man, who was pictured as speaking at the graveside of his only son, supposed to have been killed in this same war against the Turks. The father was not grieving over his son's death, but was, on the contrary, congratulating him on his good luck in being now in the presence of the great national hero Dushan, and was urging the boy not to hide his lights, but to be sure to let Dushan know at the first opportunity how brave he had been in battle, and to tell him exactly how many of the enemy he had killed before he himself was struck.

There was a strange pathos in the reflection that all that was noblest in this fine old poet, was still breathing the atmosphere of six centuries ago. The intervening years of Turkish tyranny formed a spiritual hiatus which had to be ignored by poets and heroes. It was an arresting thought too, that this old man—a type of the finest characteristics of the spirit of the Past, had sacrificed everything—work, wife, children—in order that his nation should now at last break through the darkness of those intervening centuries, into the light—such as it is—of the Western world. One couldn't help also surmising that if Dushan had not come to a sudden and untimely end, the Slavs might have federated and driven the Turks out of Europe all that long time—six hundred years—ago. My old friend firmly believed that Servia, Bulgaria and Montenegro were now, at any rate, joined in a lasting federation, and in answer to a doubt which I expressed as to whether, when the Turks had been defeated, there might not be disputes amongst the Allies as to boundaries, etc., old Tsched Schljivitsch replied enthusiastically: "No, no—Why! we are one people—we have *one* faith, *one* language—and now soon we shall be free to work out our own destiny!"

And though they are now, in deplorable fashion, working out this destiny—along the lines of example set them by Western Europe—the Allies are, in their internecine fights and struggles, only going through the inevitable process of testing their relative strengths before settling down to the work of nationhood. If only Turkey is excluded from re-entrance to the arena, the evolutionary process in the Balkans will probably soon be in full swing. Passions of territorial ambition and of jealousy have, it is true, caused the Allies in their mutual distrust to forget the first object of their crusade. But this is only temporary. The spirit of this old poet-warrior-priest was, as I discovered later, truly the spirit of the Balkan peoples. They had, at that time, all alike tucked up their cassocks, and, turning their backs on everything in life that was less dear than liberty, had gone with crucifix and rifle and memories of Dushan to the front.

CHAPTER VI

As the train drew up at Sofia the station was a nightmare of bewilderment. Every inch of platform was crowded with brown-uniformed Bulgarian and Servian soldiers, on their way to the front—wounded soldiers returning from the front—and with women who swarmed round every incoming train in the hope of finding relatives and friends. The genus porter alone was missing from this congeries of humanity, and it was a bit of a puzzle to know how to get one's luggage conveyed from the van, where it was mixed up with military and Red Cross stores, ammunition and wounded soldiers, to the Hotel Bulgaria. But after a chaotic scramble this was accomplished, and I hastened to get to work upon my mission.

Having been given an introduction to Dr. Radeff, Director of the Bulgarian Red Cross Society, and son-in-law of Monsieur Gueschoff, who was then Prime Minister, I telephoned for an appointment and received immediately a courteous invitation from Dr. Radeff to call at once at his house and have a talk. He accepted gratefully, on his own account, my offer of the services of the Convoy Corps, but said he must communicate by telephone with Dr. Kiranoff, the P.M.O.—head of the medical and military department—who was then at Stara Zagora, at that time the headquarters of the Bulgarian army. In the meantime Dr. and Madame Radeff—who both talked excellent French—most kindly offered to show me as many hospitals as I could digest, and took me that same Sunday afternoon to see, first the Red Cross Hospital established in the École Militaire, where one thousand wounded soldiers were being housed. The nursing of the wounded was, throughout Bulgaria, being supervised by Queen Eleonora—a Princess of the House of Reuss, a trained nurse who had been a sister in the Russo-Japanese War, and who not only understood the work, but was devoting herself heroically night and day to the organization of the hospitals. She was at that moment away from Sofia, at Phillippopolis, and it was on my return to Sofia, a few days later, that I had the privilege of meeting her.

The nursing at the Red Cross Hospital was in the hands of volunteer ladies of society,

A Mosque in Sofia.

who for the most part wore linen frocks and white caps and aprons, with Red Cross badges on their arms. Though nearly all were untrained and had at first been quite unused to sights of blood and horrors, they one and all gave it as an invariable experience that, though they had previously imagined they would faint at the sight of blood, they had not even felt squeamish when it came to the reality. There was no time, they said, for anything but to *work* at relieving the overwhelming mass of human suffering which was all around.

Nearly all of them had near relatives at the front, and I asked one lady, whose husband and two sons were fighting, if she had heard lately from them, and where they now were? She told me that she had not heard for ten days, and that even when they wrote they were not allowed to give the date or the name of the place from which they wrote, nor were they allowed to mention names of those who had been killed or wounded. No list of killed or wounded would be published till the war was over. "How dreadful for you," I said sympathetically, as I realized the agony of such prolonged suspense.

"Oh!" my friend replied, "but it is much better not to know! If one *knew* that the worst had happened one would grieve and that would hinder work, and there is so much to be done!—Oh! *much* better not to know!"

This same brave spirit, characteristic of Bulgarian womanhood, was also illustrated in the case of another woman—a widow—who had lost two sons in the war. The news that they were dead leaked out, and some one told her of her loss. Tears came in her eyes, but she quickly brushed them away, saying sternly, "Don't think I am crying because my two elder sons are dead; I'm crying because my two younger boys are not old enough to go and help drive out the Turks."

And it was this spirit of determination to get rid of the Turk *at all costs*—because the Turk hampered their evolvement into nationhood, that turned every Bulgarian man into a soldier, every woman into a nurse, and was the ideal which inspired them one and all to their marvellous victories. And though to the politically short-sighted the subsequent war of Bulgaria against her former allies, appears to be a relapse into barbarism and bloodthirsty and territorial greed, even this war with its disastrous consequences, is an inevitable outcome of that first so-called "righteous war." In all evolutionary processes there occur periods of mutation when a re-arrangement of the corpuscles of which the atom is composed, is essential in order to arrive at a new position of equilibrium. This adjustment of equilibrium amongst the Balkan Allies, is a necessary preliminary to further stability. The adjustment is by blood and carnage, because that is still the tribunal to which the civilized world resorts. The necessity for this particular outburst of blood and carnage might not at this moment have occurred had it not been for the intervention of the "Great Powers," who prevented Bulgaria from completing her work, and driving the Turks out of reach of a renewal of mischief, and who set up an autonomous Albania and thereby gave Servia a grievance which she could only hope to remedy at Bulgaria's expense. No one who has had a first-hand knowledge of the Bulgarian character, would believe that the Bulgars were capable of *faking* an ideal or of *dropping* an ideal which they had once visualized. And that they *had* visualized the ideal of *Freedom*—of emergence into the light of nationhood from the darkness of an asphyxiating tyranny, was, at the time I was in the Balkans, clearly shown by illustrations large and small.

CHAPTER VII

EVERY theatre in Sofia was closed, because all the actors were at the front and the actresses were in the hospitals. All the schools and colleges were closed, because the professors were in the fighting line. One professor at whose house I called with Dr. Radeff, had volunteered for service as telegraphist at the front, but because he was too valuable in his own department in Sofia, the Government had refused permission. However, when we called at his house and asked if he was at home, the servant replied in a matter-of-fact way, " No, Professor —— has gone to the war." He had apparently taken the law into his own hands, had shouldered his rifle and was now in the forefront of the fight. Probably, alas! killed in that battle—so disastrous to the professors and artists of Sofia—which took place near a village through which, later, I passed on the trek from Jamboli.

I visited also that afternoon some of the

smaller as well as the larger improvized hospitals in Sofia, and the story was everywhere the same. Splendid enthusiasm amongst nurses and doctors, but in the latter case hopeless under-manning—many of the best surgeons being at the front—and in the case of the nurses, a general lack of training and of experience. I felt that if this were the case here in the capital, any help that the Corps could give would be doubly serviceable nearer to the fighting line, where volunteers would be fewer in number. When, therefore, in reply to Dr. Radeff, Dr. Kiranoff telephoned that he gratefully accepted my offer of service, I made up my mind that our work must be as *near to the front* as possible.

I was anxious that arrangements should be definite before I cabled to the Corps, and, not satisfied with the vagueness of a telephone message, and desirous of obtaining *every form* of official sanction *in tangible shape*, I arranged to start immediately for Stara Zagora to receive from Dr. Kiranoff himself, definite information as to where and what our work would be, and what equipment would be necessary.

I had the good fortune to have been accompanied from London by my friend J—— and by Mr. Noel Buxton, M.P., and his brother Harold, who were on their way to join the Military Staff. Having all been presented with free passes and with Red Cross officially stamped brassardes, we started in a train reserved for military and Red Cross purposes, at 7 a.m., on our twelve hours' journey.

As the train steamed out of the station, the view of Sofia, inset between the snow-illumined mountains of Vitosch on the south, and the Balkan range on the north, was surprisingly beautiful. The new cathedral, with its golden cupolas reflecting the brilliance of the morning sun, spoke aloud of the aspirations of the Bulgars and of the marvels that had been accomplished during a short thirty-five years of autonomy by this wonderful people.

The journey all the way was full of tragic interest. At every station, stretchers and ambulance-carts were in readiness to convey the victims to hospitals along the lines of communication, and round each north-bound train, anxious friends and relatives crowded, eager to see if their beloved were amongst those, maimed or dying, who were being carried on the stretchers or were hobbling with improvized crutches, as best they could, to the waiting carts. Sometimes a little group, silent, with bared heads, would be carrying to the train, on his last journey, for burial in his native town, the coffined body of an officer who had died of his wounds in hospital,—had passed across the blood-filled trenches to the land of freedom.

At every station, contingents of Red Cross women attended night and day to give hot tea and bread and cheese to wounded and Red Cross travellers. We also received, and gratefully, their hospitality, for there was no other food procurable. Restaurant keepers, like all other human males in Bulgaria, were busy pouring out, not tea and coffee, but human blood.

The lines were, of course, monopolized by the military, and truck-loads of murder-spreading batteries of machine guns, both Bulgarian and Servian, and of the soldiers—uniformed in brown or in grey—of both nationalities, streamed southwards in one continuous flow. The horrors of war were vividly portrayed, for whilst the trucks going *south* were full of fine specimens of Bulgarian manhood eager to get to the front to strike for the freedom of their brethren, and shouting enthusiastically the national "Shumi maritza," the trains going *north* were full of human wreckage *returning* from the front, and on its way to the various evacuation hospitals along the line. And as the heavily freighted trains slowly passed each other at the stations, the salutations "Sbogom! Sbogom!" between those who, maimed and crippled, had already faced death, and those who were now on their way to meet whatever the fate of war might bring, must have moved the stoutest heart that was not already inured to the tragedies of warfare.

But that evening a pleasing diversion awaited us. For when we arrived at Stara Zagora—a straggling townlet, lately rebuilt for the seventh time, after having been burnt and devastated by the Turks—we were greeted by a deputation consisting of the Mayor and Prefect, and interpreters, who came into the corridor of our train to welcome Mr. Buxton, who for his services to the Bulgarian peoples is very much *persona grata* in Bulgaria.

I have heard criticisms of the Balkan Committee's efforts for the Balkan people, from those who look out on life from the prison loopholes of a narrow nationality.

"Isn't there," say these arm-chair critics, "plenty of work to be done in their own country?" But the secret of usefulness is not to wait for this, that, or the other special work to come to hand, but to treat as *our* work any

MILITARY TRAINS WITH BULGARIAN SOLDIERS
ON THEIR WAY TO THE FRONT.

work needing to be done which comes our way? And on this occasion I was particularly appreciative of Mr. Buxton's work for the Bulgarian people; for after an address of welcome to him had been read and interpreted, I came in for a share of reflected glory, and was invited with the others to a dinner which was to be given in his honour.

We were first driven in carriages to the private houses where we were respectively to receive hospitality for the night, and were then conducted to the restaurant. In addition to the Mayor and Prefect of the little town, the Director of the Medical-Military Department was, I was glad to hear, to be present with his staff, and an opportunity would thus be offered me of talking with him under favourable circumstances and arranging, as I hoped, the sphere of operations for the work of the Convoy Corps.

All this sounded eminently satisfactory, and I was much relieved at finding that Dr. Kiranoff had not already moved on to a new base. The evening promised to be full of interest.

The Mayor could speak only Bulgarian, and his conversational efforts were interpreted by a Bulgarian lady who knew neither French nor German, but only English. The officers present knew no English, but only French or German, the remarks of the Mayor had therefore to be re-interpreted into either or both these languages for their benefit. Conversation was thus a little polyglottish. But it was, of course, full of interest, centring round the incidents and events, the battles and triumphs of the latest phases of the war. And in happy innocence of coming trouble I was, in a detached way, thoroughly enjoying myself. The stage of the dinner was duly reached when liqueurs and cigarettes were handed round, and toast time arrived. The Mayor rose and proposed "England," and included in his praise of the Old Country a warm eulogy of Mr. Buxton. The latter in due course responded in the French language. All this I was enjoying—still unconcerned—when suddenly, as Mr. Buxton sat down amidst an outburst of applause, he turned to me—I was sitting next to him—and said, " I say, I think you'd better get up and say something." A thousand times rather would I have had him ask me to put my head on the executioner's block! But I answered quietly and quickly, "All right, what language had I better speak in?"

"Well—I spoke in French—perhaps you'd

better speak in German," he whispered cold-bloodedly.

"Very well," I said, as though an impromptu speech in the German language was the sort of thing I did every night before going to bed. "Who shall I speak for?"

"Oh, I don't know," he answered, "anybody —anything you like—only, hurry up."

"All right," I murmured, as the buzz of conversation around us stopped, in a horrible hush of expectation, "I'll speak for the women of England." So I did. I don't remember, fortunately, what I said, but to my surprise it was apparently satisfactory, for when I had finished, Dr. Kiranoff—his face beaming with smiles—came up to me and, shaking me warmly by both hands, said in German—

"Look here—a woman who can get up at a moment's notice and make an impromptu speech like that—in the German language—is capable of anything. What work do you want to do? Where do you want to go?"

My suit was won! I replied meekly, "I want, please, to go as near the front as possible."

"So you shall," he answered; "I'm moving on to-morrow to Kirk-Kilisse, which is about to become the headquarters of the Bulgarian army. This will be within the active zone of operations, and therefore in the more pressing need of nursing and surgical aid. You shall if you like come too, and improvize a hospital on your own. Can you do this?"

As I had already ascertained that no foreigners would be allowed by the Bulgarians in *field-hospital* work, and that there would therefore be no chance of obtaining consent to help in convoy work between field and base hospital, I of course gladly accepted Dr. Kiranoff's offer. He asked me to come to his office next morning that he might send—by telephone—instructions to the Commandant of Kirk-Kilisse. This I did, waiting all the morning for the response, which came satisfactorily at last. It was agreed that on reaching Kirk-Kilisse with the Corps, I was to present myself at the headquarters of the Commandant and receive final orders. The parting words of the P.M.O. as he saluted and wished me goodbye, were "Auf wiedersehen —at Kirk-Kilisse!"

I at once cabled home to the Corps for those members who had already been provisionally selected, to start at once for Sofia. I told them, as far as was possible by cable, the nature of the work, and that they must bring surgical instruments and appliances, stretchers and such hospital equipment as they could muster. Mr. Noel Buxton, as chairman of the "Balkan War Relief Committee," generously undertook to pay the journey expenses of the Corps members to and from Sofia. From Sofia onwards we should, as a part henceforth of the Bulgarian army, be provided for by the Bulgarian government, and as I could further rely upon the Bulgarian Red Cross store of supplies in Sofia for supplementing deficiencies in our own equipment, the road was clearing for action in promising fashion.

CHAPTER VIII

I KNEW, however, that a week at least must elapse before the Corps could arrive at Sofia. I determined, therefore, to spend some of the interval by journeying on to Jamboli, there to make preliminary arrangements for the convoy of the Corps thence to Kirk-Kilisse. For the railway line via Adrianople had been cut by the Turks, and the only way now to reach our destination would be to travel in rough bullock-waggons over the Rhodope mountains and the rolling plains of Thrace. Bullocks and waggons might now be difficult to procure, and need to be ordered in advance. Also at Jamboli I wished to take the opportunity of studying further the working of emergency hospitals, for I had guessed, and rightly, that the state of affairs prevailing in the hospitals at Sofia would be, compared to the conditions in the remoter and smaller towns, like the proverbial green tree to the dry. And so it was. The buildings were of course smaller, and in most cases hopelessly inappropriate under ordinary circumstances for the reception of wounded multitudes.

In one instance a hospital had been improvized in a building that had been, in normal times, a large boys' school—as evidenced by the pile of desks and benches heaped in a conglomerate mass, exposed to snow, frost and rain, in the yard outside. The hospital contained at the moment when I arrived to visit it, late one afternoon, 200 beds which were occupied by 250 patients—lying three in two beds placed close together—and was staffed by one surgeon and five nurses. Even working night and day, it was impossible for the wounds to be dressed more than once in every twenty-four hours. This condition of affairs was, considering the severe nature of the wounds, drastic enough, but I was present when, one evening at nine o'clock, there arrived a further convoy of bullock-waggons, bringing 300 additional wounded from Lule Burgas!

It was a pouring wet night, the men had been jolted in open springless ox-waggons, their wounds untended, for five days, and as they were carried in on stretchers and deposited on the floor of the large entrance-hall, or hobbled in on crutches which had been cut from trees by the roadside, their condition was indescribable. Indescribable also were my feelings as these men—a dozen at a time—streamed into the little surgery to have their wounds dressed, and I saw the Herculean task of those five overworked, but calm and heroic sisters, and of the surgeon who was in the operating theatre: realizing as I did that at home hundreds of skilled and disciplined nurses who had offered their services had been told that there was no work "fitted for women" in the Balkans.

Shirts and trousers were frequently glued with clotted blood to the wounds, and had to be wrenched or cut away. With 300 patients outside urgently needing to be tended, in addition to the 250 already in the wards, delicate handling was impossible. Collargol, with which in our own hospital we later, at the request of the Bulgarian doctors, experimented, with marvellous effect, had not apparently yet been introduced. The wound was simply smeared with iodine, then wrapped in white sterilized lint, cotton wool and bandage, and the patient would hobble out to spend the night wherever in the town he could find a shelter; only the stretcher-bound and those for whom walking was impossible were retained, and laid on mattresses on the floor, wherever spare corners could be found. I could not discover when, if ever, those devoted

BULLOCK WAGGON IN JAMBOLI.

women and that surgeon slept, but they were calm and philosophical, as though the conditions were not at all abnormal. Nor were they indeed abnormal, when at that time, as I was told, there were in Jamboli 8 doctors for 7 hospitals and 2000 patients.

I spent a day in making friends with the Commandant, in whose hands would rest arrangements for our convoy to Kirk-Kilisse. He was very friendly, and as his guests J. and I lunched and dined with him and his wife at the little restaurant. We watched the departure of the Buxtons, who left in a Government automobile for Kisilagatch, where—as recounted in Mr. Buxton's interesting book *With the Bulgarian Staff*—they joined the Army Staff. The next day we entrained for Sofia, where I was to meet the Corps and escort them back to Jamboli and on to Kirk-Kilisse.

The eight hours' journey took twenty-five hours, from 11 a.m. to 12 noon next day. There were of course no sleeping berths, but we had been given a carriage to ourselves. However, as the train was leaving, some military officials asked us if we would, as a favour, make room for two wounded Bulgarian officers, who would otherwise have to wait for another twenty-four hours before starting for their homes in

Sofia. One of these had been wounded in the leg, and we of course insisted that he should lie with his leg outstretched,—sleep was therefore as usual out of the question for the rest of us.

This officer had been wounded and left upon the field of battle. He heard Turks approaching and crawled down the opposite slope of the hill and hid all that night under some bushes. He was eventually found and conveyed by Bulgarian soldiers to a wayside hospital, but he had during his crawl along the earth contracted tetanus. Now in Bulgaria, tetanus is regarded as an infectious disease. As soon, therefore, as it showed its usual symptoms he was removed from the ward in which he had lain, and placed in a small dark room by himself. Here he was neglected, and but for the help given by a devoted soldier servant—a comrade who had fortunately only been wounded in the arm and could therefore move about and bring him food and look after him—he would undoubtedly have died. All this, the officer told us, was unknown to his young wife, who had not even been told that he was wounded. His return would be to her a surprise. He was afraid, he said, to shock her by cabling to her now, and he was wondering whether she would be at home when he arrived, or perhaps be away visiting her parents in some inaccessible country place. He and his comrade, who had been wounded in the arm, told us ghastly incidents of atrocities which they had seen committed by the Turks upon the battlefield.

Stories of atrocities must, of course, be accepted with reserve. But it is not unreasonable to assume the possibility that cruelties will be committed by a people whose religion enjoins not only scorn and contempt, but wholesale slaughter, also even mutilation, of the unbeliever. It is proclaimed in the eighth chapter of the Koran as a precept of holiness: "I will cast a dread into the hearts of the unbelievers. Therefore, strike off their heads, and strike off all the ends of their fingers; this shall they suffer, because they have resisted God and his apostle."

But after all, our own ancestors were still worshipping Odin in the eleventh century, so we cannot brag overmuch.

Our wounded officers had much of realistic interest to tell us of the various battles in which they had taken part. In one charge which they graphically described, they told us how the Bulgarian cavalry had cut down the Turks as though they were "slicing cucumbers." They also told us, and this was later confirmed by all the patients in our own hospital, that the Turk dreaded the bayonet more than anything else, and everywhere the same quaint story was told in explanation of this dread. It was apparently due to a misinterpretation of words. For the Bulgarian words of command for the bayonet charge are, "Na pred na nosch." But the Turks, with an indifferent knowledge of the Bulgarian language, understood the command to be, "*Po* pet na nosch." This means, "Five on one bayonet"! And the Turk, objecting to overcrowding on the bayonet, rather wisely adopted the alternative of flight.

The time passed quickly while we listened to the Arabian Night stories of the adventures of our friends. The night was also diversified by frequent stoppages for the disembarkation, at stations, of the wounded. Once, in the middle of the night, as our train steamed slowly out of a station into the darkness, we passed a train going south, heavily laden with batteries of Servian guns and crowded with Servian soldiers on their way to help in the attack on Adrianople. Suddenly a great shout of "Sbogom! Sbogom!" (the Bulgarian and Servian salutation) vibrated along the length of both long trains, and, looking out, we saw in the other train the open doors, the roofs of the trucks, and the windows of the carriages, all crowded with sturdy, sunburnt Servian peasant soldiers; while at our own train windows and open truck-doors appeared simultaneously the ghost-like forms of men—white-faced, mutilated—with bloodstained, tattered garments. Both train-loads—of whole and of wounded—jostling each other for front places, all alike eager to catch a sight of comrades in a common cause, and cheer for deeds done and to be done. Our own two wounded officers had jumped up at the magic sound of "Sbogom," and before they could be prevented, the lame one had hobbled to the window of the outside corridor, and was waving both arms and shouting as loudly as his weakness would allow; whilst the other, not satisfied with waving his one remaining arm, had seized his comrade's crutch and was enthusiastically waving it out of the window, shouting with all the strength that he could muster, to swell that never to be forgotten sound of "Sbogom! Sbogom!"

But the journey, long enough eventually for all of us, came to an end at twelve next day. Before we parted from our officer friends, who persisted in thinking we had helped to make them comfortable, they made me accept, as a token of their gratitude, a mother-of-pearl electric lamp which one of them had carried in his pocket throughout the war. At Sofia station they were helped out of the train by Sanitaires and were borne off by friends, and were soon indistinguishable amongst the usual seething mass of soldiers, stretchers and stern-faced women who crowded every platform.

CHAPTER IX

My work during the next few days, whilst I awaited the arrival of the Corps, was well defined. I must buy or loan everything in the way of hospital equipment on which I could lay my hands. Mr. Buxton had, on behalf of his committee, put a sum at my disposal, and the Croix Rouge would, I knew, give all the assistance in their power. Meanwhile Queen Eleonora had now returned to the Palace from Phillippopolis and her tour of hospitals along the line, and she very graciously sent me a message through Monsieur Delmard—Director of the King's Botanical Gardens and Major Domo at the Palace, who had been very kind and helpful to me in many ways—that she wished me to come and talk to her about the Corps and our proposed work at Kirk-Kilisse.

Accompanied by Monsieur Delmard and Dr. Radeff, I therefore went to the Palace and was received by the Queen in her own private room. She spoke English perfectly, and appeared much interested in all I told her, and patted my hand approvingly as we talked. She would like, she told me, to make the acquaintance of the Corps, and hoped I would arrange for them to spend a night at Sofia on their way to Jamboli, that she might see them, and that they might have a rest after their long journey. Then turning to Monsieur Delmard, she told him he was to let me have a large consignment of blankets, shirts, sheets and bed-garments which had just arrived for her from England, and she also requested Dr. Radeff to help me in every way he could. I left the Palace feeling that the Bulgarian nation were very fortunate in possessing this particularly capable and practical Princess as their Queen. There was no red tape or affectation of any sort about her. She was full of insight, intuition and human sympathy. I had the privilege of seeing her and talking with her at the Palace twice again, and each time I confirmed my first impression, that her charm to me, at any rate, consisted in the fact that she was not a royal automaton, but a real live woman.

And now my way was clear, for Dr. Radeff generously put the store-rooms of the Croix

STREET IN SOFIA, SHOWING (AT THE END OF THE STREET) ONE ENTRANCE TO THE ROYAL PALACES.

NO WILD
INVENTERS

Rouge at my disposal, with permission to take any equipment I desired. I accordingly selected blankets, bed-linen, crockery, pots, pans, knives, forks, spoons, etc. to my heart's content. I now had—taken in conjunction with equipment which the Corps would bring —everything I was likely to be able to get, except beds. And beds—of a portable nature —were, I was informed, unprocurable, having all been requisitioned for the existing hospitals in Sofia and elsewhere. But beds I must have, so I took no notice of the pessimists and began a systematic hunt in unlikely places— the likely places having presumably all been emptied of contents.

For two whole days I was unsuccessful, but finally on a deserted wharf I came upon some suspicious-looking packing cases, from one of which was projecting something uncommonly like the leg of an iron bedstead. I therefore fetched some workmen whom I saw in the distance with some tools, told them to unfasten the wooden case, and lo and behold! the usual miracle! which always comes when faith and will are backing an Ideal. The packing-case, and many other packing-cases, contained between them seventy-five light portable iron bedsteads, which any of the hospitals in Sofia would have given their eyes to possess—iron bedsteads which henceforth were mine! For no sooner had the first case disclosed its treasures than the owner—by the help I supposed of my magic wishing carpet—suddenly appeared, and I commandeered, against payment, the whole lot—exactly the very beds I wanted. And now all I had to do was to arrange for mattresses and pillow-cases of sacking, which would all eventually be filled with straw, to be prepared. Also I must procure some interpreters, not only to translate the wishes of our future patients, but to help us on the journey.

I was particularly fortunate in securing the services of four young men, two of whom were English and spoke Bulgarian, whilst two were Bulgarian and spoke English, and also two Bulgarian girl-teachers who spoke excellent English. All was now in readiness for the arrival of the Corps. I knew nothing of the size of the hospital nor the number of patients we should be given to treat, but as I had procured all that was procurable in the way of hospital necessaries, and I knew that the Corps would also bring all they had been able to collect under Miss Streatfeild's able superintendence, things would probably work out all right. In the recipe of that delicate dainty "success," the heavier ingredients of organization and will-power, must be lightly whipped with "faith" to taste. In this case, at all events, things worked out in the most marvellous fashion. For, on receipt of my cable, my second in command, and officers of the Corps in London, contrived within a week to collect from friends £600. With this money they purchased surgical instruments and appliances, blankets, stores, and other equipment, a perfect supplement to that which I had been able to requisition in Sofia.

And now at last the Corps were due to arrive and, with all arrangements completed, I had the satisfaction of welcoming to Bulgaria the first company of women who have, as a self-contained unit, set up and administered a hospital of war within the zone of active operations.

CHAPTER X

THE unit numbered sixteen, and included, besides myself as Commandant and Directrice, two Sisters, Miss V. Adams and Miss P. Gadsden, four other fully qualified trained nurses, six members for general duty as cooks, dressers, nurses, etc., and the three women doctors, Dr. Alice Hutchison, Dr. D. Tudor and Dr. E. Ramsbotham. Of the splendid services which these three doctors rendered to the wounded, and of the spirit in which they took all the rough and tumble of the expedition, I cannot speak too highly.

The contingent arrived without mishap at Sofia. They had expected from my earlier instructions, before I knew of the royal command, that they would be travelling straight through to Jamboli. But hand baggage was quickly collected, the heavier luggage and equipment left in the van, to be found again at Jamboli, and the whole party were conveyed to the Hotel Continental. Here our friend

Dr. Radeff had kindly arranged for their reception for the night.

The effects of the four days' and nights' continuous journey without sleeping-berths, were soon obliterated by a wash and a good breakfast, and the morning was spent in seeing the town, though the public buildings were, of course, in consequence of the war, all closed. In the afternoon Mons. Delmard most kindly himself conducted the little party over the Royal Botanical Gardens and the Greenhouses of the Palace. Then at 7 p.m. we all met at the Hotel Bulgaria, which is just opposite the Palace, and were here joined by Dr. Radeff, who accompanied us on our visit to the Queen.

At the Palace we were met by Mons. Delmard, and were shown into an ante-room which formed one of a long suite of fine big rooms with parquet floors, and walls hung with oil portraits of King Ferdinand and his ancestors, of his first Queen Marie Louise of Bourbon and of their four children, Prince Boris, Prince Cyril, and the Princesses Eudoxie and Nadezda. Also, of course, portraits of Queen Eleonora.

We waited a few minutes and were then ushered into a larger room beyond. Here the members formed up in line, in readiness for inspection by the Queen, who, dressed nurse's uniform, soon appeared. She first received me and made many kind inquiries as to how the members had fared on the journey from London, and as to the arrangements made for our farther journey next day to Jamboli. Next I introduced to her our officers, and then Her Majesty spoke to the members as they stood in line, and asked each in turn to describe to her the special work for which she was prepared. She showed great interest when Mrs. Godfray, as Cook-in-chief, explained that the Corps cooks were trained not only to work in well-equipped kitchens, but that they learned in camp to dig their own camp-fire trenches, and to build of mud and turf, their own chimneys and fireplaces, and were thus independent of conditions. This very much pleased Queen Eleonora, and turning to one of her ladies-in-waiting she said: "Ah! what an excellent thing it would be if our Bulgarian ladies went through this training!"

And then Her Majesty gave attention to our uniform, on which she bestowed much praise. It struck her, she said, as being eminently practical and workmanlike. It consists of Norfolk jacket with large concertina pockets, full skirt, which divides back and front when required for riding—either sidesaddle or astride—and pith helmet hat, all made in a greeny grey tweed material. Shirts are of white silk for officers and of white cotton for the rank and file, in ordinary times; whilst in camp and on active service, as at that moment, all wear flannel shirts of a colour to match the uniform. The principle upon which the uniform had been selected was *serviceability in the field*, and it has admirably answered its purpose, though there is too much skirt. For work in the hospital and for cooking, washable linen frocks and white caps and aprons are worn.

The question of uniform has never been to me unimportant. For I believe that "clothes, despicable as we think them," are, as Teufelsdröckh remarks, "so unspeakably significant." It is, as a rule, precisely those who devote the most time and money to clothes, and who wear clothes that are in every sense extravagant, who have least appreciation of their value as symbols. Women who shrink from wearing in the street, anything which betokens a uniform, are not as a rule afraid to wear garments which, if they represent anything at all, are representative of Ideas that are unnameable. The shrinking from wearing clothes which are distinctive of an *Idea* means a shrinking from acknowledgment of that Idea. The desire on the part of women to wear something that will not be discovered as a uniform means a half-hearted belief, or none, in the *Idea* behind the uniform, or it betokens lack of faith in the capacity of the Public to recognize an Idea. *Is* there an Idea, a distinctive Idea, at the back of your work—whatever it may be?—then that Idea must be represented by clothes. If the Idea has truth and honesty and soundness in it, the clothes will savour of truth and honesty and soundness. They will not be outrageous unless the Idea at the back of them is outrageous. If then there is a sound Idea at the back of the work which women are to do in warfare, it must be symbolized for the public, as the Boy Scout Movement has been symbolized, by a distinctive uniform—a uniform which, without being in any sense extravagant, is readily recognized and speaks for itself as representative of *work*, not of dolldom or half-heartedness. Women will never, as a sex, do useful work till they wear clothes which are appropriate to work, and—though this may come as a revelation to many—there is no physiological reason against this. "The essence of all science," says Carlyle, "lies in the philosophy of clothes."

Queen Eleonora had the wisdom to observe

that our uniform, though possibly not becoming to good looks, was very becoming to good work, and she thoroughly approved. Her Majesty then, after she had walked down the line and talked with each in turn, including of course the doctors, in whom she showed great interest, told me to disband the members and let them disperse about the room. The two young Princesses, step-daughters of the Queen, were also present. They were about fifteen and sixteen years of age, and looked very charming in white Princess frocks, made quite plainly, except for some beautiful Bulgarian embroidery on the yoke. They were also "to the manner born," and moved around amongst us all, and talked to everybody in English, understanding excellently how to make even the shyest feel at ease.

They themselves were too modest to tell us, but the Queen mentioned that they also were taking a share in the work of alleviating the overwhelming burden of national suffering, and every morning with their own hands these little Princesses baked bread for the wounded soldiers and took it themselves each day to the hospitals.

Finally, the Queen, before she left, expressed again to me her gratitude for our goodwill and proposed services to her soldiers, then she and the Princesses gave to each of us signed photographs of themselves, also packets of chocolate for the journey, after which, bidding us Godspeed, Her Majesty left us. After a little further conversation with the Princesses, the ladies-in-waiting, Mons. Delmard, Dr. Radeff and the officers-in-attendance, we departed, feeling that a motive of loyalty and personal affection for Bulgaria's Queen would now be added to our motive of loyalty to our own cause, and give additional zeal and enthusiasm to our work of nursing the soldiers of the Bulgarian nation.

The next morning, when we arrived at six o'clock at Sofia station, we found awaiting us a courier from the Palace. He had been sent by the Queen with a kind message of farewell, and also with a large case of provisions for the long train journey to Jamboli. There was no time then to write a letter of thanks, but we arrived at Phillippopolis that afternoon. The train stopped for half an hour and we were met by the British Consul-General and his wife (Mr. and Mrs. Wilkie Young), who came to the station to greet us, and most kindly offered any assistance in their power. I was then by their kind help enabled to dispatch my telegram to

THE PRINCESSES EUDOXIE AND NADEZDA OF BULGARIA.

the Queen without the usual delay and bother of long hours of waiting at the Censor's office. The half-hour went all too quickly whilst we talked—over glasses of tea, served in Russian fashion, with slices of lemon and no milk—in the crowded station-room with Mr. and Mrs. Young, about their good work of organization of relief for the families of the soldiers, and of the general prospects of the war, etc.

We were sorry not to see more of Phillippopolis, a beautiful little town named after Philip of Macedon, and ideally placed amongst five rocky hills. But after this point the interest of our journey was intensified. For we were now drawing near to Jamboli, and, instead of taking the usual southerly route via Adrianople to Kirk-Kilisse, it was necessary, as the Turks had cut this line of rails, to travel eastwards via Stara Zagora to Jamboli, and thence traverse the Rhodope mountains and the Thracian plains, a seven days' trek in the ubiquitous bullock-waggon.

As our train drew up at the little ramshackle town of Jamboli, at midnight, in pouring rain and pitch-black darkness, I guessed we should thenceforth have need of all the resourcefulness at our command.

To my relief I found that, by order of Dr.

Radeff, the Croix Rouge had kindly arranged for officials to meet us with automobiles and convey us and our hand baggage to night quarters at the Roman Catholic Convent Hospital, about two miles from the station. Here we were hospitably received by the Sisters of Mercy. We slept in wards lately occupied by wounded soldiers, and early next morning, in the chapel ante-room, we breakfasted on tea without milk, the hard brown bread of the country, and white sheep's milk cheese.

And now the task before us was to procure ox-carts—forty it was reckoned would be needed for ourselves and the equipment—eighty oxen or buffaloes, and forty drivers, and make a start that evening if possible. But it was still raining in torrents; we were two miles from the station, from which the start must be made, owing to the heavy luggage; the cars of last night had vanished, been requisitioned elsewhere, no conveyance of any sort was available, and the mud was in places knee deep. Everybody who had ever, at any time, known anything about anything, had " gone to the war," and if by chance, with one's Bulgarian interpreter safely pinned to one's side, one ever did find the right person who was likely to be able to give information as to carts and oxen, etc., that "right person" invariably turned out to be a Greek or a Turk who couldn't understand Bulgarian, and one had to begin all over again.

It is true that my friend the Commandant had, on my previous visit, said I was to let him know when I returned, and that he would help me to get all I wanted. But when, after considerable difficulties, I succeeded in running to earth the Commandant—behold!—it was a different Commandant—who knew not Joseph, and had never heard of the Convoy Corps. He was very kind and sympathetic, and the contrast between this stolid Bulgarian and my impetuous English character might have been interesting to psychologists. But I was not out for psychological study, and it was distinctly troublesome to find that nothing whatever had yet been done towards procuring the large number of bullock-waggons we required. For to me, every hour's delay in getting on the move, was of fatal importance. On the one hand, we were still separated by seven days from the place where lay our work, and if the war were to end before we arrived our journeyings and labours might be, I feared, in vain. On the other hand, the Bulgarians had swept the Turkish forces victoriously before them along the route we were to follow—*up to the present*. But if the tide of battle should unexpectedly turn in favour of the Turks, and the Turkish army were to roll back and re-take the Thracian battlefields over which we had to pass! . . .

I was fully conscious, in the secret recesses of my own mind, of this latter risk, and indeed the Turks have since returned step by step across our trek. But unless one acts in commonplace moments upon the inspiration of one's more valiant moments, nothing of value is ever achieved. And nothing that is worth doing is ever accomplished without some risk. I was on Mahommedan territory, and I felt, as Mahomet once had felt, that "if the sun now stood on my right hand and the moon on my left" ordering me to desist, I could not obey. The risks only stimulated resourcefulness and determination to push on with all speed, and before the day was over all obstacles had been overcome, eighty oxen and buffaloes were being yoked to forty carts by forty Bulgarian and Turkish drivers, and all that now remained to be done was to procure provisions for the trek.

We had been told that this would be a

simple matter, that there was no need to bring food from Sofia, that Jamboli would be able to provide us with all the food we should require en route to Kirk-Kilisse. An interesting bit of mythology quite unfounded on fact. We found that every atom of food there may ever have been in this straggling village had already been consumed by the thousands of transport drivers who had from the beginning of the war traversed this same route to and from the front.

The kind Commandant and his kind wife both did their utmost and accompanied us in our raid upon the shops. But "when we got there the cupboard was bare," and so the poor Corps had none. The only result was two half-loaves of sour brown bread, two small tins of sardines, and a couple of hundred precious eggs. The usual reassuring labels "eggs new laid," "eggs equal to new-laid," "eggs," were all lacking, and we had to take on trust, eggs that, for aught we knew, might not have been laid within the memory of man. Within the memory of *woman*, those eggs are likely not to be forgotten for many a long day. They will thus enjoy immortality at both ends of their existence. We had, however, no choice but to rely on optimistic assurances that we should be able to supplement our larder at Kisilagatch and at other villages through which we should pass. More mythology! For it was a case all the time of, "if you are passing, you can—pass."

But à la guerre comme à la guerre. Nothing was of consequence compared to the fact that our tumbrils were at last all loaded—twenty-eight with luggage and equipment, and all we had now to do was to stow *ourselves* away—two in each of the twelve remaining carts, fasten the Bulgarian flag—red, green and white, to the leading cart, for we were now a part of the Bulgarian army—and get away!

CHAPTER XI

It was four o'clock in the afternoon, and the rain was still falling steadily when the little cortège began its seven days' trek across the roadless plains and mountains of Rumelia and Thrace. We had been provided with an escort of two soldiers and two policemen, who walked beside us with fixed bayonets. The carts, small and narrow, were springless and without covering, except for an inefficient straw mat, slung to little purpose across the top. The draughts, therefore, when at night it froze, or rained, or blew a hurricane, were of an interesting variety. The sides of the carts sloped to a spinal ridge in the middle. In *theory* this was covered with hay or straw, commandeered en route, whenever it was procurable. But in *practice*, the oxen invariably ate the bedding by day, with the connivance of the drivers, who could not otherwise get enough fodder for their starving cattle. Sleep therefore for two, even lying sardine fashion, heads and feet alternately, was a little difficult.

Each cart was drawn by either two white oxen or two buffaloes, and was driven or led by peasants, of whom about two-thirds were Bulgarian and one-third were Bulgarian Turks. My driver Pietro was a splendid fellow, typically Bulgarian, dignified, silent, always courteous and obliging. He owned about forty acres of land, and because he was a taxpayer was not bound to serve in the army. He was, however, taking his share of national service by working for the army transport.

Some of the drivers walked obligingly alongside, in the mud, which was sometimes up to the axles of the carts; others insisted stolidly and somewhat sulkily in sitting, according to their usual custom, on the front of the cart, indifferent to such trifles as to whether or no this necessitated their squatting on the feet of their inside passengers when the latter were trying to sleep.

It was the duty of the escort to direct the route and to keep in order the scratch crew of drivers, who, being composed of Turks and of Bulgarians, were liable to give trouble. But each nationality kept to its own camp-fire at night, and cooked its own food separately, and

PIETRO WITH MY BULLOCK WAGGON.

on the whole all behaved excellently. Once one of the drivers had a narrow escape from being bayoneted for insubordination. The oxen had been, of course, all through the war, wretchedly overworked and underfed, and one evening, when our guides desired, after a long day's trek to push on for another span, this driver refused to take his weary oxen any farther. He, however, hurriedly changed his mind when he saw the gleaming bayonet of one of the soldiers making straight for the middle of his heart. He gave no further trouble. This escort-soldier told me he was going "to the front" as soon as he had done his work with us. He was longing, he said, to have a thrust at the Turks, because in 1877, during the Russo-Turkish War, they had murdered his father and mother before his eyes and left himself for dead.

The first night's outspan was not idyllic. We had started late, rather than be delayed for another day, and owing to the abnormal condition of the track, which could not at that point be manœuvred in the dark, we were obliged to halt for the night on ground which had been trampled into a quagmire, feet deep in mud and ordure, by the many thousand oxen which had preceded us across Thrace to the main seat of the war. The night was coal dark, and rain was still falling, when we outspanned and set to work to try and light a fire to boil a kettle and cook some eggs, before settling to sleep in our ox-cart beds. The conditions were in every way so thoroughly disgusting, leaving no loophole of alleviation, that I was thankful. For the mud in which we had to puddle about was so deep and the state of our skirts and boots and putties, became in a few minutes, whilst we searched for wet wood, so abjectly ludicrous, that the situation could only be treated as a huge joke. And from that point of view we all agreed that we hoped never to encounter for the remainder of our lives, anything more humorous. The impossibility of lighting a fire by which to cook food, made the absence of food to cook, a godsend, and the joy of moving off at five next morning from our mud and manure midden, more than compensated for past inconveniences.

Joys are relative, and this little experience greatly accelerated our pleasure when, after a three hours' trek, we outspanned on some grass by the roadside, where in comparative luxury we could boil a kettle and experiment on those *prime-evil* eggs.

WOMEN'S CONVOY CORPS ON TREK.
Showing some of the Escort.

Our route lay—via Kisilagatch, Dervent, Siliolo and Jenergi—through about fifteen small villages. Of these villages some would be inhabited by Bulgarians, even in territory which had before the war been Turkish, others by Turks. It was with some keenness that on arrival at Kisilagatch—the first possible source of food supply—we set out marketing. But food in quantities was unprocurable here as elsewhere, and we considered ourselves in luck's way when, at the end of a tour of the tiny hamlet, we found a room which in ordinary times would have been a butcher's shop, and which was now the last resting-place of one small undefinable lump of pork. This we seized unceremoniously, together with a small iron grille which was lying by chance upon the counter. I wanted the grille, and the owner generously presented it to me as a present. We only found otherwise a few loaves of hard brown bread and some sheep's milk cheese. But sufficient unto the day must be the food thereof. Many more people die from overfeeding than from lack of food. We quickly adjusted our standard of requirements to circumstances, and were therefore quite content. As this was the largest village we should pass through on our route, a supper of even this unalluring lump of hog's flesh would probably in future, loom in imagination as a legendary luxury.

Except for this piece of pork, there was nothing remarkable about Kisilagatch, unless it were the women. They dressed in garments beautifully embroidered by themselves, and all of them, even to the tiniest girls, carried little spinning machines, which they worked as they walked along, — as though they were unconscious that a war was raging all around them, and that hosts of armies had passed through their village and eaten them out of house and home. I understood later—by comparison with other villages through which we passed—their apparent unconcern, for with the exception of the raid upon their food supplies, this village had been left unimpaired.

Beyond the frontier it was unusual to find a village which had not been either burned or devastated by the Turks, or been deserted for fear of the Turks. The whole of that portion of Thrace was a depopulated wilderness. Time after time, when with renewed hopes we approached something which had from the distance looked like a possible living village, we would find deserted ruins and derelict homes. The only sign of life would be a starving troop of skeleton dogs and cats, with still enough life

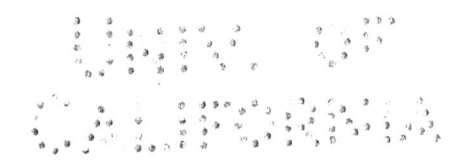

TURKISH AMMUNITION CARTS CAPTURED BY THE BULGARIANS
AT THE FRONTIER VILLAGE OF DERVENT.

left to crawl out and petition us for food. Only here and there had a village been spared, and on arriving at one of these rare oases, it was the duty of our soldiers and policemen to secure for us as much bread and cheese as they could commandeer.

The houses, when there were any left, were picturesquely made of sun-dried mud, with terra-cotta tilings, and with stoeps or verandahs—Dutch fashion—to serve as shelter from the sun and rain. On one rare and fortunate occasion we had been able to make our midday halt at one of the small villages which was still more or less intact. A Bulgarian peasant woman opened the door of her hut, and came outside to look at us. As it was raining I asked her if she would allow us to eat our bread and cheese under the friendly shelter of her stoep. She agreed, and then went back into the house, to go on with her work, and closed the door. We in the meantime laid out our Spartan meal upon the stoep, and lighted a fire in an adjoining shed, to boil water for our precious tea. Another woman, with a baby in her arms and three small children clutching at her skirts, had been standing on the stoep watching us in silence. I asked her if she lived here, and she then told us that she did not belong to these parts, that she came from a village near Adrianople, and was now, with her children, being hospitably sheltered in this two-roomed cottage by our hostess, who was her cousin. Her husband and her father had been captured by the Turks, to be transport drivers of oxen, and were now besieged in Adrianople. She did not expect to hear their fate till the war was over. I wanted the woman inside to come out and join us in our talk, and I opened the door, and, standing on the stoep, called to her. She was making bread, and two small children hid shyly behind her skirts when they saw me: while two more were lying asleep, Turkish fashion, on a mat upon the floor. The woman had mixed the dough in a long trough and was now putting the bread—which she had fashioned into long loaves—into the oven, built in the Dutch fashion of bricks, and heated with wood, the usual fuel. The bread looked excellent—a thousand times better than the stuff made by soldiers with which we had often to be content, and I praised it. The woman shook her head.

"We've no salt," she said,—"that has all been taken by the soldiers."

"But all the same, it looks lovely," I answered, and—thinking of my starving Corps

WOMEN'S CONVOY CORPS CROSSING THE
BULGARIAN-TURKISH FRONTIER.

Univ. of
California

—"I should be glad if you would sell me some."

"I'd rather be killed," she answered curtly, "than let you have this bread. It's all I've got—my children would die—their father's fighting." She turned round sharply—" Look at them, can't you see they're starving?—one died last week—and those"—she glanced towards the children on the stoep, then stopped. She had caught sight of our soldiers outside, and knew they could commandeer the bread. Other soldiers had taken all she had last week, and had given her nothing for it. "You can't have it," she ended abruptly, and shut the door upon me.

And for the first time I realized a grim reality that was subsequently often enough impressed upon me—that one of the cruellest results of the wars men wage upon each other, is the sufferings of the women and children. Men take all these sufferings for granted, and in dispatches no mention is made of the heroism shown and the tortures endured by women—by mothers for their starving children. It is an evil thing that men only should witness the results of war. Wars will never cease till women—at whatever cost to themselves—are admitted behind the drop-curtain, and discover, amongst the cardboard scenery and the grease-paints which glorify for the public the tragedy of war, the brutal realities which are the secrets of those behind the footlights.

And now these villages have all been revisited by the Turks—and what will have become of those two brave women and their children?

We of course left them their bread, and trekked on over country that, taken as a whole, reminded one alternately of the rocky hills of Dartmoor, of the rolling veldt of the Transvaal, or of the plains of Salisbury. But a black silence brooded over the whole country, which seemed mutely, sullenly, to be protesting against the stupendous folly and neglect of man. For though Nature had created a fine country, with agricultural opportunities offering happiness to all, man had made of it a black Sahara. There were no roads, only tracks over old ploughed and pasture fields and neglected vineyards from which some of the famous "Bordeaux" wines are grown. Occasionally we passed through woods of oak and beech-scrub, stunted, as everything under Turkish rule is always stunted. Everywhere for years, trees had been cut down ruthlessly for fuel, and nowhere was there visible any

A Thracian Well, with Bulgarian Peasants.

UNIV. OF
CALIFORNIA

sign of replenishing the fast vanishing stock of timber.

It was impossible to read or write in the carts, owing to the jolting, in and out of the ruts worn deep in mud, trampled by the thousands of bullock-waggons which had preceded us, conveying soldiers and military stores to Kirk-Kilisse and the front. Sometimes we would amuse ourselves by walking beside our carts for a few miles, where the mud had dried a little, and it became imperative to stretch cramped limbs, though great care had to be taken that there were no stragglers left behind.

Water was not very plentiful, and the outspans were apparently not determined, as in Africa, by the supply of springs or lakes, and sometimes the halt would be made in a place where no water at all was procurable for boiling our kettle for tea, the one luxury that was left to us. We grew wary, therefore, after a bit, and kept over—treasured in bottles —a supply of water from each place where there had been no scarcity, for an emergency kettle This indifference as to the water supply on the part of the drivers was probably due to the fact that they themselves had no fads either about the necessity of *clean* drinking water or the necessity of drinking at all, and if they ever were thirsty they would stoop down and drink contentedly from the mud puddles in the road—over which myriads of oxen had passed. If godliness and cleanliness are inseparable, we were indeed a most unholy company, for washing—except an occasional lick and a promise of hands and face, was out of the question, for we passed no rivers, only one spruit, and the only available bathing water was from village pumps or wells. We began to understand what a slum child feels when at the beginning of the winter it has its clothes sewn on. Ours never left our backs for eight days.

Our average pace was one and a half to two kilometres an hour—exasperatingly slow, in view of our anxiety to get to work. Sometimes, however, the monotony of the day would be relieved by passing over a battlefield, from which we could collect relics, and from the disposition of the trenches, reconstruct in imagination the main incidents of the fight. At one place—upon a plain which extended as far as the eye could reach—the Turks had evidently, whilst encamped, been taken by surprise. They had obviously decamped in a great hurry, for the field was

Bulgarian Peasants spinning and reeling Yarn.

strewn with remains of Turkish tents and their peculiarly-shaped tent-pegs,—with shirts, trousers, papers, torn pages from the Koran, cartridge-cases, bullets, Turkish music—belonging to the band—something of all sorts indicative of an encamped army, scattered broadcast over a mile or so of plain. One could almost hear that famous Bulgarian war-cry, "Pet Nonosch," and see the Turks scampering scarified over the plain towards Kirk-Kilisse, in front of us.

Our routine each day was much the same. As soon as day dawned the soldiers would arouse the drivers, who had spent the night lying round their respective Bulgarian and Turkish camp-fires, then the oxen which had been tied all night to the carts in which we were supposed to be asleep, would be inspanned, and a trek of two or three hours, according to the nature of the country, would be made, before a halt was called for breakfast. Our cooks would then collect firewood and light a couple of fires, boil the water for tea, and proceed to "cook the breakfast," a valuable euphemism which was diligently upheld. After a couple of hours of outspan we would jolt on again for another three or four hours, then halt again, and so on till nightfall, when we would "cook supper" and go to bed, thankful that another day was passed and we were by so much nearer to our work.

"Going to bed" was always an event of interest, owing to the uncertainty as to whether there would be any "bed" in the shape of straw to lie on, or whether, whilst we were at supper, the drivers would have taken it for their oxen. On the first night of the trek I was going the round of the carts, to see that all was well, when, as I came up behind the cart of one of the senior and most circumspect of the party, I heard an exclamation of a surprisingly unparliamentary nature. I knew something serious must have occurred for such an outbreak from such a quarter, and with some anxiety, as I came round the corner, I inquired what was the matter?

"I'm sure it's enough to make a saint swear," came the answer,—"the oxen have eaten *all* my bed!"

I laughed, and then the bedless one laughed, and never once during the whole trek, or indeed from the start to the finish of the expedition, did I hear a word of grumbling or of discontent at any of the privations or inconveniences which were encountered by any of the party. Not even when on one occasion, having by a

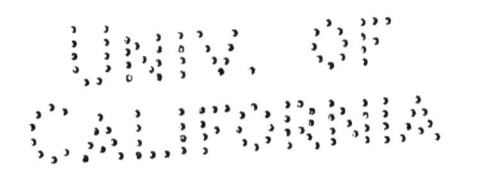

MY OX, JUST AFTER HE HAS EATEN MY BED.

UNIV. OF
CALIFORNIA

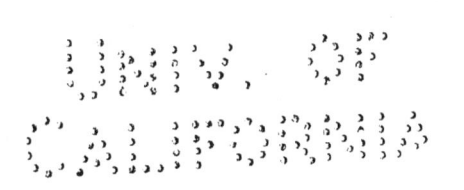

CONVOY CORPS ON TREK—BREAKFAST OUTSPAN.

UNIV. OF
CALIFORNIA

miracle secured, just before we turned in—too late for that night's supper—two precious chickens, it was found in the morning that one had been eaten during the night by a starving cat.

This was at a Turkish village, then in possession of Bulgarian soldiers. Most of the inhabitants had fled, and the Bulgarian soldiers were guarding Turkish prisoners of war, who were being made to work, and were not, apparently, enjoying the new experience. In this village we were rationed with bread made by soldiers—unaccustomed to the task—for themselves and for their prisoners, and though eventually the bread had to be eaten, to keep the wolf from the door, we had every reason for believing that the local stores of bullets and of loaves had inadvertently got mixed, and that we had been served from the wrong locker. We quite understood why the Krdzaligen of old demanded "tooth money" or dyschak for the wear and tear of their teeth on the hard bread of the peasants. A sense of humour was dished up as *hors d'œuvre* at every meal and filled many a gastronomical blank.

CHAPTER XII

But we had one red-letter day. Having grown accustomed to finding the villages, when we arrived, either burnt to the ground or deserted, and to being met by skin-and-bone dogs and cats which ravenously begged of us food we could ill spare, we could scarcely believe our ears when we heard one evening as we approached a village, the joyous sound of a crowing cock! Promptly the soldiers were called and told to find immediately and raid—against payment of course—that cock-roost, wherever it might be. Within a few minutes the escort returned triumphantly with half a dozen already slaughtered fowls. And that evening we had roast chicken for supper. We had no cooking pots, but we threaded the six fowls on a long stick supported on either side of the camp-fire by two iron rods taken from one of the ox-yokes, and we hungrily enjoyed what was for us a rare feast. There was no bread sauce, but appetite sauce was a wonderful substitute. And whilst we ate, the villagers—mostly women—(Bulgarians) gathered round us, talking with heroic resignation of the destitution which stared them in the face. They all, as usual, had blood-curdling stories of rapes and mutilations committed by the Turks upon their fellow-villagers. Amongst the group was one man who was a priest, and another who was in ordinary times a school-master. Both seemed particularly alert and intelligent, and I asked them how they accounted for the extraordinary success of the Allies over the Turks.

"Ah!" they answered, "we Bulgarians always knew the war must come, and we had predicted the result. How," they argued, "could it be otherwise? Every man is a soldier and every soldier owns his bit of land, therefore every soldier is fighting for himself as well as for his country and his fellow-countrymen. And the Turk—what does *he* fight for? The *country* is nothing to *him*. He conquers with the sword, but he never settles or mixes with the conquered races."

"Yes, but," I said, hoping to draw on my friends, "though you Bulgarians fight for your *country*, the Turk fights for his *faith*. Is not that as powerful an incentive to deeds of valour?"

The priest smiled scornfully. "Faith? The Turk has no longer a faith,—and that is why he loses battles. A soldier who believes that if he dies fighting he will go straight to Paradise, *might* think it worth while to kneel for twenty-four hours at a stretch up to his waist in water—and blood—in the trenches,—one thing against another!—But the young Turks have been to Paris—*that* is now *their* Paradise, and they don't get there by staying in blood-filled trenches. *We* are fighting to free ourselves from a tyranny we can no longer bear. We have an Ideal before us. The Turks are only fighting to keep up a condition of affairs which is unjust. They have no Ideal—they will never beat us!"

Then these peasants told us stories of the battle which had taken place around their village. For it was here that the flower of the professional world of Sofia had been destroyed, here that the wayward professor upon whom Dr. Radeff and I had called had, as I surmised, been killed.

That was a memorable evening. We had outspanned on a high plateau, surrounded on two sides by rocky hills like those of Dartmoor, and commanding to the south-west an extensive view over the vast plain in which Adria-

Convoy Corps on Trek — A Midday Halt.

nople is set. As the crow flies, we were not far distant from the besieged city. Of this we were reminded by the continuous booming of the besieging guns. Our imagination had not been blunted by the brutalities of war, and for us that was a nerve-racking sound; for we knew, though not a word was said, that every rumble of those cannons and every flash of those spiteful fires as they blazed from the cannon's mouth into the darkness, meant brave men killed, or worse still, maimed and shattered, and homes made desolate.

And all that evening searchlights swept the sky, and penetrated the recesses of our oxcarts, and, as an additional reminder that we were now well within the area of war, the peasants pointed and told us where even now at this moment there were lying the corpses of many Turks still unburied, and the lightly covered bodies of those many brave Bulgarians who had perished in battle around this village.

My driver Pietro told me that with his people it was the custom to put a lighted candle and some food upon the grave, a month after death, and that they dug the grave shallow and tacked on the lid of the coffin very lightly, so that the dead might get out if they felt inclined. But those poor dead who were around us that night were not cumbered with coffins. They were, however, mercifully hidden from us by the darkness, and to make up for time lost over the broken axle of a cart which we had been obliged that day to leave by the roadside, the oxen were inspanned next morning whilst it was still dark, and we started on trek before dawn.

The Bulgarian driver is, compared to the Kaffir boy, strangely noiseless, and the only sound as the little procession moved off into the darkness was squish, squish, as the wheels of the swaying carts forced their way through the quagmires of mud which marked the track. There was no moon, and the stars, weary with what they had seen of the ways of men, disappeared from view one by one, and left us to the darkness "between the two great Silences."

And now that the big guns were quieted for the few hours of night, there was, over all the world, a peace—that peace which passeth all understanding, the peace which precedes the dawn. And then away in the eastern horizon, the blackness gave place furtively to a faint grey light, which spread slowly and reluctantly till all the world was grey. Ah! there was no help for it—the day must come!—I glanced

A Devastated Village between Jamboli and Kirk-Kii SSE.

back along the grey outline of that little procession—in single file—of our ox-carts, and wished I could have painted my impression of the picture revealed by the light of that grey dawn.

Grey carts, white oxen, led in silence by Bulgarian and Turkish peasants—also grey and white, with their grey clothing and white navushtas—defiling between the grey rocks of a narrow gorge, and freighted, not with Turkish or Bulgarian merchandise, but with British women who, themselves emblematic of the dawn of a new day, had, without thought of fear or of discomfort, thrown off the shackles of civilization and were jolting peacefully towards a Turkish town, there to render service to those in need.

Betwixt Odalisque and Women's Convoy Corps what an interval!

We were now nearing our journey's end, and on the evening of that day a glad surprise awaited us. We had already outspanned for the night in a particularly unsavoury farmyard in the little village of Jenergi, garrisoned at the moment by some 500 troops. I was looking round with a hopeful eye for chickens when an officer came up and, saluting, brought a message from his C.O. inviting us all to come into the little café and have a cup of coffee. The invitation, though kind, didn't sound *very* nourishing, but we gratefully accepted, and crowded into the tiny room, about twelve feet square, which had been cleared of soldiers who were smoking and drinking, to make space for us. With eyes fixed upon a dark inner room, from which supplies might not unreasonably be expected to emerge, we all sat round two long empty tables, whilst the officers, evidently glad of a little social diversion, stood round and chatted with us.

There was probably a hungry look in our eyes, for in a few minutes the truth—I'm thankful to say—leaked out, that we were starving, and with one accord the officers insisted that we must eat the soup which had just been prepared for the evening meal, and was now about to be served in their own quarters close at hand. I *think* I tried to remonstrate, but was horribly conscious of half-heartedness, and in a few minutes plates of delicious-looking soup, full of thick chunks of meat and vegetables, were being offered us by those blessed officers and their orderlies.

I shall never forget the sudden silence which followed the placing of those plates of soup upon the table in front of us.

We remembered that meal intimately, for it was the last we had, worthy of mention, till we arrived at our destination two days later.

In our impatience to get to work, those last two days seemed interminable, but even at the rate of one and a half kilometres an hour, the trek, which had lasted seven days, came to an end at last, and our cortège drew up—as usual in a manure yard—outside Kirk-Kilisse (called by the Bulgarians Lozengrad, the town of the vines), each one of us eager to start upon our mission.

CHAPTER XIII

IT was one o'clock when the oxen and buffaloes were unyoked in the mud-trampled encampment by the side of the road, on the outskirts of the town. My business now was to find the Commandant and receive orders—to find also, as I hoped, my good friend Dr. Kiranoff.

The drivers were told to wait in camp till my return, and I, together with the senior doctor and the senior sister and an interpreter, marched off into the town. It was, I was sorry to know, Sunday, and the office of the Commandant might possibly be closed. We discovered his headquarters and found that he was away! "Was the P.M.O. in the town?" "No—he was away at Chatalja!" For a moment my heart sank. Had *no* work then been arranged for us, after all? I decided that the Commandant must at all costs be unearthed. I could not contemplate losing half a day before getting to work. I was besides anxious to get the Corps away from that foul encampment before night, if possible.

"Where," I asked, "was the Commandant?" Cross-examination disclosed the fact that he was, as I suspected, lunching at the military club,—"he would return later." But I had my doubts about that return, as it was Sunday. We therefore went to the military club.

This was very carefully guarded, and there was some difficulty in persuading the sentries to let us through. But we were finally admitted to the entrance hall, and I was able to send a message to the Commandant, who was, I was thankful to find, under the same roof!—He sent a courteous reply that he would return at once to his office, and hoped to see me there in a few moments. We returned, therefore, and before long the Commandant was safely in my presence.

I asked for orders. These were simple. We were to go through the town and select for ourselves any houses we thought suitable for conversion into hospitals, and set to work at once. There were thousands of additional wounded hourly expected from Chatalja, and help would be sorely needed.

I had expected that perhaps the buildings would have been already selected, but I of course acquiesced without comment "And if," I asked, "the houses we should select should chance to be inhabited—what are we to do?"

"Turn out the inhabitants," was the answer.

"All right," I replied, as though it were part of my daily routine to walk through Turkish towns turning the inhabitants out of their own houses. "But before we start to work, could you direct us," I asked, "to a restaurant? We're a little hungry, and I want the members of our mission to get some food as soon as possible."

He very kindly sent one of his officers with us as guide, and told him to take us to the best restaurant in the town. The guide, who talked very incomplete French, took us through narrow, muddy, irregularly cobbled streets to this "best restaurant" Alas! the shutters were up and the place closed. But our guide knocked at the door. For some time there was no reply, but eventually, in response to a fist-cannonade from our united forces, the door was opened and a surly-looking man, apparently—as our guide informed us—a Greek, muttered some words in a language none of us understood, pointed to the shutters, shrugged his shoulders, and shut the door in our faces.

"It's Sunday, and feeding time is over," said

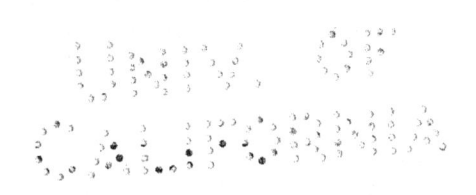

Kirk-Kilisse from the South.

the guide laconically. " But we'll try elsewhere."
We tried at every " elsewhere " in Kirk-Kilisse,
with the same negative result. "I'm sorry,"
then said our guide, " but I can do no more.
You must wait till to-morrow. Adieu!" and
he left us.

But I had no intention of waiting till to-
morrow. I pictured all my comrades in the
carts eagerly waiting for us to return and conduct
them to the promised land of food and plenty. I
was glad things looked so desperate, for I knew
this would be the moment for the miracle.

And—the miracle, of course, happened
straightaway. I glanced down the street,
wondering what to do next, when lo and
behold!—just appearing round the corner and
now marching straight towards us, with that
free and easy swing so suggestive of power and
self-confidence, two officers dressed in our own
blessed khaki uniform!

" Do ask them to help us," whispered one of
my companions. I knew these officers would
understand. So I went up to them, explained
who we were, told them we were anxious to
select our hospital buildings before night, but
wanted to have some food first. Would they,
like angels, help us to get this?

" I should think we would," replied emphatically the taller of the two, who turned out to be the British Military Attaché.

"Why, certainly—right here,"—corroborated the other, who was the American Military Attaché. And I knew all would be well now.

They went back to the first "best restaurant," and knocked as we had knocked. With the same result, a surly face, a finger pointing at the shutters, and shrugged shoulders. "You refuse to give these ladies food?" inquired our friends. "You have——?" But they were talking to closed doors. "All right," muttered the officers, "you're up against something different this time, my friend. We'll soon see if you'll provide food or not." Our attachés straightway went back into the main street, which was swarming with soldiers—soldiers on their way to the front, soldiers wounded returning from the front, soldiers, soldiers everywhere—and collected at haphazard half a dozen stalwart specimens. The British Attaché then gave the command "Fix Bayonets," returned with his escort to the restaurant, stormed the door, forced it open, and made the soldiers stand inside with their bayonets fixed, ready for action. "Now, will you give these ladies food—or not?" asked our British officer quietly of the restaurant keeper.

With eyes fixed uneasily on the gleaming bayonets, the man replied sulkily, " We would if we had it, but we've none left—it's Sunday—it's all finished."

But from my position at the door I'd been looking round, and my eyes had spotted a cupboard underneath the counter, " But what," I asked, " have you got then in that cupboard? I'm sure you have *eggs* there "—I sniffed loudly,—" I can *smell* eggs in that cupboard."

" Open the cupboard," commanded the officer.

It was full of eggs!

With the bayonets pointing at him the restaurant keeper was made to take out some eggs, and, followed by the soldiers and the bayonets, the attachés and ourselves, our host proceeded to the kitchen, where the eggs were very promptly converted into omelettes. And I can guarantee that " omelette a la bayonette " is a dish for epicures.

The officers stayed with us while we lunched, and kindly invited us to have tea with them later at their quarters, then, after I and my companions had sent word to the Corps to come up and get some food, we returned to the office of the Commandant, ready for anything.

The task before us was simple. We were

given an official guide who knew the town and had a list of the commandeerable houses, and we set off on our errand. The mud was in places a foot deep, and, together with the painfully irregularly projecting cobbles, demanded, under ordinary circumstances, careful steering with eyes upon the ground. But I was wearing long, practically heelless rubber boots, which were mud and cobble proof, and I was able, though with difficulty, owing to the crowded condition of the narrow streets, to keep critical eyes upon the houses on either side as we walked along.

I came to the conclusion, after the first five minutes, that unless the outside of those dirty, impossible-looking houses belied their interior possibilities as hospital wards, the Commandant must be playing a practical joke upon us, in telling us to select houses *suitable for hospitals*. I less and less appreciated the idea of having presently to dive into one of those uncanny-looking interiors and turn out the inmates neck and crop.

But it was no good shivering on the brink—the plunge must be taken. "I wish to enter that house," I therefore told the guide, as I saw through the open doorway of a small courtyard, a dingy, unsavoury, tumble-down house on the other side of the quadrangle. It was, I thought, at least a *little* bit away from the street.

"Ah! yes, that was a Turkish hotel, and very suitable," our guide thought. We accordingly crossed the little yard and ascended a dark, narrow staircase leading up to the house itself. We opened the door of the best room the house contained. It was about ten feet square with low ceiling—no fireplace or ventilation—the windows were closed, an iron stove was burning fiercely, and from twenty to thirty Turkish soldiers were squatting, playing cards or lying asleep, on the floor. The dirt and the smells were a revelation of possibilities.

"These are Turkish prisoners; they can go elsewhere if you want the house," intimated the guide.

"Thank you, but I shall not be wanting this house," I replied. But for educational purposes we looked over the other rooms and inspected the (save the mark) sanitary arrangements. Then, having received our first never-to-be-forgotten lesson in Turkish sanitation, we emerged once more, thankfully, into the outer air, realizing that our British standards would have to be considerably readjusted if we were to succeed in adapting ourselves to Turkish environment.

The remainder of the afternoon provided us with a varied experience of Turkish interiors, each house we entered seeming to be a little more unsuited for our purpose than the last.

We had entered and discarded as impossible, house after house, with no prospect apparently of anything more suitable turning up. It was therefore now obviously time for the miracle. The best, I told myself, was being kept as a surprise till the last. And so it was.

Suddenly we entered a side street looking quite different to the rest The street, though as usual nameless, was a little broader and more airy, and the houses were modern and comparatively new. Almost at once we pounced upon two houses, one-storied, facing each other on opposite sides of the street, as suitable for our purpose as we were likely to find. They had been private houses occupied by Turkish families, as evidenced by the harem casements and the crescent over the doors, and must have belonged to people who were well-to-do, for there were good-sized entrance halls downstairs, and some of the rooms were comparatively large.

The only present occupants were some

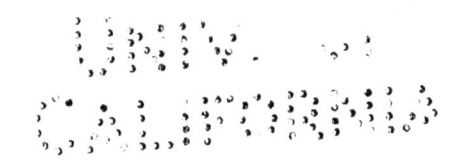

WOMEN'S CONVOY CORPS HOSPITAL—HOUSES LEFT AND RIGHT OF FLAGS.
The House on right contains Operating Theatre.

convalescent soldiers thankful to find even the shelter of an empty house. For it contained nothing of any sort but dirt. We told the soldiers they must turn out to-morrow at sunrise. It was too late, unfortunately, now to start on the Augean cleaning task. As these houses would not contain the staff, who were in any case better separately housed, we searched further, and found in an adjoining street another empty house in which we arranged to put up bedsteads for ourselves.

Hugely thankful at the result, in the end, of our afternoon's work, we made our way back to the famous restaurant to arrange, as we grandly hoped, for supper for the party. But once more we found that we were too late. At such short notice the restaurant people, though quite polite, could not give food to so large a number. But we had secured our hospital building, and nothing else mattered in comparison. We therefore went to our good friends the Military Attachés to tell them the result of our afternoon's work and to get our promised cup of tea. They were just going out to dinner at the military club, but they gave us tea and biscuits, and then most kindly rummaged their lockers and found odd tins of meat which they generously insisted on our carrying with us to the camp. So we returned to the rest of our expectant party, lighted our fires and ate our supper—sitting on the shafts of the ox-carts—on ground that was, in spadish language, a manure heap. In spite of all disadvantages, however, we were all full of hope and good spirits, for to-morrow our real work would begin.

CHAPTER XIV

THE next morning at daybreak all was astir in the little camp. Our escort had disappeared, but some of the Corps remained to superintend the inspanning of the oxen, which were to convey luggage and equipment on their last short stage to the doors of the hospital, whilst the remainder took in charge the cleaning of the hospital houses. The Commandant put at our disposal during our stay in Kirk-Kilisse a young Infantry lieutenant, then convalescent from wounds received during the war. He spoke French, and his duty would be to requisition for us all that we should require in the way of food and other necessaries. We were also presented with a dozen Bulgarian soldiers and reservists, to act as orderlies for carrying water, scrubbing, digging trenches, or for doing any odd jobs for which our small staff could ill be spared.

Before the work of cleaning the hospital houses could be begun, however, water, pails, cloths, scrubbing-brushes and soap had first to be procured. The water supply in a pump in our backyard was too impure, we were told, to be used for any purpose. We had therefore to seal the pump and find water elsewhere. We fortunately discovered some in the yard of a house farther down the street. Pails—well, there were none in Kirk-Kilisse, and empty paraffin tins had to be found and converted into water carriers. Cloths we made hurriedly out of sacks from which blankets and stores were being emptied; and scrubbing-brushes and soap, the lieutenant, when he arrived, was able to requisition from somewhere, and the work was at last set going.

The soldiers had obviously never seen a scrubbing-brush before—a broom made of twigs for sweeping dust being the nearest approach to a floor-cleaning weapon with which they were familiar. The amazement on their faces when they were told to follow our example and go down on their hands and knees and use water, brushes, soap and cloth, was worth watching.

The larger of the two houses, destined to be the main hospital, contained on the ground floor a large entrance hall. From this there opened on the right, a room used by me as an office and place in which to receive officials and visitors to the hospital. The kitchen opened out of the hall at the farther end, and a scullery beyond led into the backyard. On the left side of the hall and near the entrance doors was the surgery and out-patients' room; a tiny store-room lay beyond, and beyond that was a small room used at first as a dining-room by the staff. We eventually deserted this room, because it was permeated with essence of cesspool which stagnated just outside the window, and we screened off a portion of the outer hall as a mess-room.

Upstairs there was a broad corridor which made an excellent ward, and was always full, not only with bed-patients, but with others who had to lie on straw mattresses on the floor, the beds being all in use; and the four rooms which were used as wards, also a surgical store-room, opened into this corridor. There was a Turkish lavatory upstairs, and one downstairs, but of course no bathroom. The stairs were circular, and particularly ill-adapted for the conveyance of stretchers.

The house opposite was more or less similarly arranged, and contained a bright, good-sized room which we used as a theatre for operations.

As we had been warned of the possible early arrival in Kirk-Kilisse of a large convoy of wounded from Chatalja, we made superhuman efforts to be ready for them; and simultaneously, whilst some of the party attended to the cleaning arrangements, scrubbed the floors and scoured the walls and the ceilings, others unpacked the huge cases of blankets, bed-garments, linen and stores, which were unloaded from the ox-waggons, whilst the cooking staff prepared the kitchen, the sisters arranged the surgical necessaries in readiness for immediate use, and the doctors prepared the surgery and out-patients' room.

On that first night the restaurant-keeper had graciously vouchsafed to give us supper,—due notice having been given; for our own kitchen arrangements were of course not yet in working order, and after supper we were more than ready for bed. But beds were not ready for us. Some of the light portable iron bedsteads brought from Sofia had been duly carried to our sleeping-house, in which we had four unfurnished rooms. But at nine o'clock the straw, ordered for filling the mattresses, had not arrived, and we were preparing to sleep upon the bare floor when, behold !—as usual—the miracle.

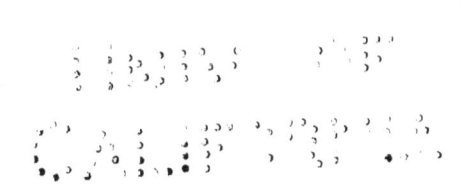

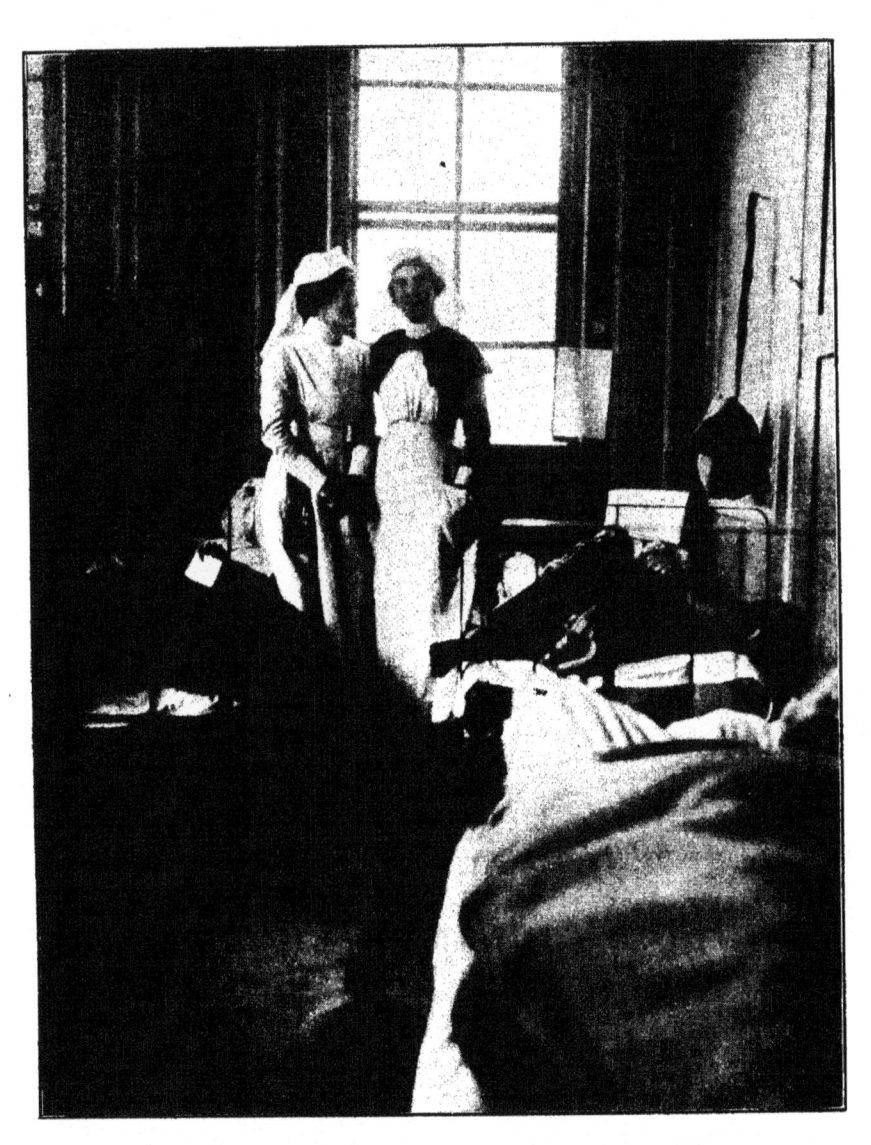

ONE OF THE WARDS, WOMEN'S CONVOY CORPS HOSPITAL.

Unbeknown to us, and whilst we were supping, Mr. Noel Buxton and his brother, who had returned to Kirk-Kilisse after their interesting tour with the military staff, went off "on their own," and just as we were arriving at our night-quarters to "go to floor" in the empty house, these two splendid people arrived at the door in the shafts of carts which they had themselves dragged full of straw—from somewhere!

Then everybody helped everybody else to fill their mattresses and pillows, and after half an hour's exhilarating scrimmage in the dark—for Turkish streets are never lighted—we retired to what might have been, but for rats, the best night's rest we had had for many a long day.

There were not even packing-cases for use as bedroom furniture—these were all needed in the hospital, but we learnt to do excellently without such superfluities.

We could also have done without the rats, which waited until, tired out, we fell asleep, and then darted out from their holes and ran about, not only over our beds, but also—bold libertines—over our faces. Their motives were, however, as we soon discovered, obviously pious, for we found them running off with such few treasures—soap and toothbrushes—as we possessed. Thus in Scriptural fashion they took from those who had not, even that little which they had!

But we had no time to worry over trifles such as rats. Early the next morning we eagerly resumed our hospital preparations.

We had immediately realized the importance of establishing *at once* an out-patients' department, for already rumours of the new hospital had spread, and the narrow street was crowded not only with curious onlookers, but with bandaged soldiers with wounds of every variety, who crowded round the doors clamouring for treatment, which the other hospitals in the congested condition of affairs were unable to provide.

With splendid enthusiasm the three doctors set to work to get the surgery going, and before the first day was over, the wounds of some dozen of the more clamorous had already been dressed, and on the afternoon of the second day, whilst the cleaning of the houses was still in progress—whilst piles of packing-cases in the halls were being emptied, then carried into the backyard and converted into benches and tables—whilst blankets, sheets, crockery, surgical necessaries, stores, etc. were

SOME OF THE WOMEN'S CONVOY CORPS HOSPITAL STAFF.
The three doctors in the centre.

being distributed for surgery, ward, kitchen or for personal use—whilst beds were being carried upstairs and fixed—whilst sack-mattresses were being made, the ends sewn up, a slit cut in the middle, straw inserted and the slit sewn over—whilst all this was still going on, seventy-one out-patients were treated in the Dispensary.

And on that same afternoon, just before dusk, ox-waggons drew up at the doors with five severely wounded soldiers craving admission as in-patients. They were suffering respectively from complicated fracture of the femur and from general bullet wounds, and one from tetanus. Though all was still in confusion, these men could not be refused, for was not this emergency work the work we had come to do?

With lightning rapidity a ward was prepared, iron bedsteads fixed, and beds made with new blankets and white sheets and pillow cases, and by the time the carts were unloaded and the stretchers had been safely carried up the stairs, the sisters, in their neat linen frocks, white caps and aprons, their Bulgarian Red Cross badges on their arms, were waiting in the wards with everything ready to receive their first patients. Thus, within forty-eight hours from the time of the arrival of the Convoy Corps in Kirk-Kilisse, their hospital was a "going concern."

It was dark at five, but the work of unpacking and sorting and cleaning was continued by those who were not needed in the wards, by the light of candles stuck into bottles, as no oil was available, and lamps could not yet be requisitioned. It was nine o'clock that evening when a halt was called for supper. The Buxton brothers, who had looked in to offer help, were with us, and we had just sat down to a meal of bully beef, in our smelly little dining-room, when I was summoned to the entrance hall.

There stood an official with the familiar Red Cross badge upon his arm. He saluted, then, pointing outside into the darkness, said: "We have here fifty wounded soldiers. They have come in springless ox-carts from Chatalja—their wounds have been untended for six days. Can you take them in?" We moved to the door as he spoke, and down the unlighted street, and dimly definable in the darkness, stretched, as far as the eye could penetrate, an unbroken line of ox-waggons. They were now stationary, the leading waggon drawn up in front of our hospital door. The drivers had dismounted and stood beside their oxen, patiently waiting for orders. Nothing was visible of the freight of human wreckage *inside* the waggons,—all was silent underneath those wicker hoods.

But I knew that fifty human beings, huddled together in horrible discomfort, were—in suffering and torture—mutely appealing to us to help them.

"Can you take them in?" repeated the Red Cross official.

"Of course I can," I replied without hesitation,—"that's what we're here for."

I knew we were not, in the strict sense of the word, "ready" for them. But our rough improvised comforts would at least be better for them than their present deplorable condition.

I knew also that the admission to the wards of all these seriously wounded men must, in the present state of our arrangements, entail a heavy strain upon our little staff. But I knew that reliance could be placed on their loyalty to their cause—which is the cause of the sick and wounded—and that zeal and enthusiasm would pull them through.

I went back to the dining-room. "There are fifty seriously wounded soldiers outside. They have come—six days—in ox-carts from

Chatalja. They are waiting for us to bring them in " was all that had to be said.

Mr. Buxton, who knew that everybody had worked without ceasing for two days, with no time to recover from fatigues incidental to the seven days' trek, remonstrated in vain that I should be overtaxing the strength of the staff. The logic of man had no chance against the intuition of woman. The doctors with fine spirit said they would tackle it, the sisters, nurses and cooks corroborated, and in a moment the supper-table was deserted and everybody was in the street taking a share in the work of conveying the wounded men from those cruel ox-carts to the wards.

During the rest of our lives none of us will ever probably again be as "busy" as we were during those next few hours.

For the carts must be unloaded and the wounded must be quickly diagnosed and distributed, appropriately to the nature of the wounds or the fever from which they were suffering, and placed under the care of doctors, sisters, nurses, orderlies and interpreters, in the various wards of the two respective houses; whilst inside, the nurses hurriedly fixed iron bedsteads and filled mattresses with straw. The removal, without injury, of the badly wounded over the immovable tailboards and front pieces of those particularly inappropriate ox-carts, on to stretchers, by dim candlelight, was no easy matter The darkness added greatly to the difficulty, for nothing could, of course, be elicited from the patients as to the nature of their wounds without the interpreters, who, at critical moments, would be whisked off to attend to some other urgent case, and be hopelessly lost in the crowd of soldiers and curiosity-mongers who as usual collected and added to the general hubbub.

But the most serious consideration was a lack of straw for the mattresses. We could manage without a sufficiency of beds, if we had enough mattresses to put upon the floor. The straw that had been ordered and promised had not arrived, and at 9 p.m. it was not likely to turn up. There was, I knew, nothing like enough straw to give each man something soft to lie on.

This was desperate. Straw must, by hook or by crook, be instantly procured. I saw an official with an intelligent, sympathetic face, standing amongst the crowd, looking on idly. I took him by the coat sleeve.

"Look here," I said, in one language after another till I found one which suited him, "you see all these wounded—they are your fellow-countrymen. We *must* house them to-night. We have no straw for mattresses. Get some, for mercy's sake!"

He nodded and went off, and I thought all was well. I only learnt afterwards that a Bulgarian *nod* means a negative—a shake of the head an affirmative!

A few minutes later I saw, standing on the same spot, an official whom I thought was my late friend. There apparently he still stood— having done nothing, and straw this night we must have. I spoke with some heat.

"This is *really* too bad—have you done *nothing*? Where to goodness is that straw?" I remonstrated. "Can't you *see* the urgency— you promised me faithfully—you"— and looking up into his face, which was a long way up, I saw that by the dim light I had made a mistake. This was not my former friend! From under the curled and dark moustachios on a handsome face, a voice replied with haughtiness, in the Italian language: "Madam, it is not one of my duties to fetch and carry straw!"

"Why not?" I replied impatiently. "Who are you?"

He smiled. "Madam, I am the Italian Military Attaché!"

"Oh! that is splendid," I said, much relieved. "I thought you were only an ordinary man, but as you hold such a high position of authority you will be able to help me all the better. You see all these wounded, they *must* have straw for mattresses to-night—it is late—and, except by a miracle, such as *you*—we——"

"Madam," he interrupted, "straw you shall have, if there is any within ten miles of Lozengrad! I haven't the slightest notion how straw is made or where it comes from, but—I am at your service."

He moved off with a business-like air, and the straw, by his orders, arrived soon afterwards. There can be no doubt whatever that military attachés are an excellent institution. No war must ever be without them.

War correspondents too, when they're not corresponding, are likewise good inventions. The correspondent of the *Morning Post*, Mr. Fox, who chanced to be walking down the street, lent us a kindly hand, and was of great assistance in helping us to carry in the wounded. The Buxton brothers, who had themselves been working hard all day in the Bulgarian hospital, were also invaluable, and within a couple of hours, that freight of human remnants, shattered in legs, arms, heads, everywhere, had all been removed from the carts and carried on stretchers or hand-seats up the inconvenient staircase to the different wards. Here the sisters took the patients in charge and distributed them—the more severely injured in the beds as far as these were available, and when these gave out, the weary wounded were placed on sack-mattresses in the halls, corridors, outhouses, in every available space, and their tattered, bloodstained garments, which were often glued to the wounds, were removed and put in bundles and numbered for subsequent recognition. Wounds were then dressed, and the soldiers, clothed in new bedshirts and linen drawers, and safely tucked up in comfortable sheets and blankets, enjoyed, before settling for the night, good plates of soup which the cooks had cleverly managed to produce.

Thus before the end of the second day in our improvised hospital, our wards were not only full, but overflowing, and the work of the hospital was in full swing in all departments.

CHAPTER XV

Two of the patients were Turks. These were, when first admitted, very nervous. One of them, looking round cautiously, whispered timorously to the nurse: "When are they going to kill me?" Though the question was capable of an alternative interpretation, we took it as an inference of the treatment likely to be bestowed by his own nation on his enemies. But he soon became friendly, and later played games of cards with his ward-mates quite happily. And from that first night any doubt which may ever have existed in my mind as to the wisdom of allowing British women to nurse and doctor Bulgarian and Turkish soldiers was dispelled. The men, both Turks and Bulgarians, gratefully acknowledged that never before had they been so well or so carefully tended; whilst our own doctors and nurses declared that, amongst the many whom they had treated at home, no patients had ever shown greater courtesy, chivalry and delicacy than was shown by these Balkan peasant soldiers.

The following day a further contingent of wounded was admitted, and I was fortunate in being able to find, a few yards farther down the street, another house which was empty and unoccupied except for waif and stray soldiers. It was therefore immediately annexed and cleaned, mattresses were placed upon the floor of the four good-sized rooms, and the house was thenceforth used as an overflow hospital for the less serious cases.

The theatre already looked very neat and business-like. It had been fitted with an operating-table and a couple of instrument-tables made by two slow-handed old Bulgarian carpenters who were commandeered for our service, and who, it must be confessed, worked only under compulsion. But our own staff could not now be spared for outside work, and there were many carpentering jobs which were essential for the comfort of the patients.

The question of ventilation of the wards was a crucial one. The soldiers had an ingrained horror of fresh air, and determinedly closed every window or door immediately the nurses' backs were turned. Remembering how I had adversely criticised the atmosphere in some of the other hospitals I had visited, I made up my mind that something drastic should be

GROUP OF SOME CONVALESCENTS, DOCTORS, NURSES, ORDERLIES INTERPRETERS.
The Lieutenant and Cook-in-Chief on right.

U.S. DEPT. OF
AGRICULTURE

done. This resolution was brought to a climax on the second day, when a particularly gangrenous-smelling wound was being dressed. The patients had as usual remonstrated at the open windows, and for the moment, while the dressing was going on, these had all been closed. I therefore opened one of the sash windows twelve inches at the bottom, summoned the carpenters, showed them a plank which I had measured and sawn, and told them to nail this across the opening—"to shut out the air," and to do the same to all the windows of all the rooms in all the houses. It is, of course, a well-known plan, but the soldiers, unaware that ventilation was secured by the free passage of air between the upper and lower sashes, imagined that the piece of wood had been thoughtfully nailed across to keep out draughts, and they were gratified. In any case they could no longer shut the windows, and my object was attained! Unfortunately, I found that some of the windows in some of the rooms were constructed on a different plan, and the little ruse seemed frustrated. For half a moment, when I discovered this, I was checkmated, but a suggestive broom with a nice long handle, stood near, and, after sending someone to make sure that there was nobody in the street below, I "swept the cobwebs" from the upper panes, and the broom clumsily went through the glass! Glaziers—a particularly patriotic class—were of course all at the front, so those windows—wasn't it tiresome—never *could* get mended.

But the question of sanitation was to me of most serious concern. It is impossible here to describe in detail the difficulties which had to be conquered. Turkish sanitary arrangements, when seen for the first time, are, under any circumstances, enough to make curled hair stand on end. But commonplace horror was intensified by the fact that we were housing seventy to eighty people in houses intended for the accommodation of a couple of dozen. There were no drains, but a thoughtfully planned pipe carried the excreta from upstairs, past the bedroom windows, down the wall of the house to a cesspool into which you could step from the dining-room window. For it lay snugly just alongside and underneath, and was only partially covered with rotten planks left loose purposely for convenience in removal. New cesspools had occasionally to be dug, and as this was not a job for which there was overdue competition amongst the soldier orderlies, nor one which they understood, it was necessary to stand over them and direct them as to the length and breadth and direction of the channels, etc., and face the typhoid foe as they themselves would face the Turk. But the discipline was, as I told myself, wholesome, even though that word were not strictly applicable to the process. *All* situations are interesting, if you can either feel their significance or see their humour. When significance and humour both stare you in the face life is a regalement.

But in addition to cesspools, trenches had of course to be dug in the small backyards for kitchen refuse, and dirty water and other purposes. The orderlies were unaccustomed to so many invidious distinctions, and constant supervision was therefore necessary. This was the more important because all refuse-carts and scavengers were "at the front," and one was obliged literally to "keep one's own stye clean."

The disposal of soiled dressings was also for the first few days a little troublesome, as they would not burn in the open trenches during the rain, and in any case the yard was too small and the odour too noxious for the process— so near the house—to be desirable. But I obtained leave to build a brick incinerator on a piece of enclosed vacant land a little farther down the street, and this considerably relieved matters.

For the first fortnight it was impossible to leave the hospital even for a quarter of an hour. There was more than enough to do in organization and in co-ordination of the various departments, which were all under-staffed for the work in hand. It was necessary also to be on the spot in case of eventualities. The arrival of new cases necessitated nearly every day re-adjustment of the wards. The more seriously wounded must be given beds in the main blocks, whilst the less serious cases would be sent to Block C as convalescents, or possibly be put on the list for return, either to their homes in Bulgaria—or to the front. Very soon too, a fourth hospital house became necessary, and for a time we were housing, feeding and treating ninety-two in-patients in addition to the out-patients. This was as many as the staff could undertake, for unfortunately most of them—myself excepted—succumbed to slight attacks of fever, similar in character to what used to be known as low fever, and were in turn incapacitated for a week or ten days at a time. But their illnesses were thoughtfully arranged to take place in succession, and as more than two were never at any given time *hors de combat*, the work was at no moment disorganized.

The authorities had kindly put at my disposal a young Bulgarian student to act as secretary. He was, in normal times, newspaper correspondent at St. Petersburg, and talked French. For the names and regimental numbers of the sick and wounded, together with the nature of the wounds or sickness, had to be registered for official purposes. Also notification and lists had to be made of those who were sufficiently recovered to be sent again to the front, and of convalescents who could be returned to their homes. All this, together with any official correspondence which might be necessary, was of course conducted in the Bulgarian language, of which the letters are written like the Russian—in Cyrillic characters, a mischievous invention of Cyril and Methodius in the ninth century. The Bulgarian language is not difficult to learn, but there was no time just then for mastering linguistic technicalities. Besides, if you *learnt* the Bulgarian, or indeed any other human language, you weren't much "forrader" in Thrace. It only prolonged the agony of inarticulation. I once, for instance, addressed, in my best Bulgarian, a woman, who, clothed in the garments of a Bulgarian peasant, was standing near me in a shop. In response she turned her head away! Much disappointed, I looked to the shopkeeper for an explanation. He then told me—in French —that this woman, though she always *dressed* like a Bulgarian, was *really* a Greek, but that she could *speak* only Turkish! "Concentrated essence of Tower of Babel," I muttered in despair as I left the shop.

Amongst other duties one had, in the office, to sign all the requisition orders for meat, bread, vegetables, firewood or other necessaries, and be at hand in case of emergencies. The question of the safe arrival—in time for the men's dinner—of the bread and meat and vegetables, caused every day moments of dramatic tension. On occasions, when dinner-time had come and some important ingredient of the dinner was still delaying, it was comforting to the cook to have someone to come to who was supposed to be able to "do something." There wasn't really anything to be done on such occasions; but time passes quicker if something is apparently in operation, and one could flutter wings and fly around, and send messengers dashing in all directions.

Sometimes, if things looked extra desperate, and a day of fasting seemed imminent, I would go round the wards with sticks of chocolate (which had been presented to the Corps), and remind the soldiers that there happened to be a war going on outside, and that little inconveniences of that nature had a tendency to make bullocks and sheep a little slow on trek, and bakers—who were all working under military régime—a little casual in their routine. And by that time the food would have arrived, the dinner would be ready and the reputation of the hospital saved.

But as a rule all went on oiled wheels, though shopping was a little impeded by a somewhat unusual concatenation of circumstances. Kirk-Kilisse is a tiny town with only about half a mile of shopping area available—even before the war. But within this small area most of the previously existing shops were now closed, because their Turkish owners had fled; whilst of those still open, some were kept by Greeks, some by Bulgarians, some by Jews of *various* nationalities, and some few again by Turks. With the result that in every week there were at least *three* Sundays—three separate days, that is, on which, either the Mahommedan, or the Jewish, or the Christian shops would be closed. But further, as each religion had of course in addition—special to its Church—its own fast days, on which days *also* its shops would be shut, and as no shop was ever open between twelve and two, or before nine or after four, when it was dusk and respectable people were supposed to be indoors, shopping in Kirk-Kilisse was somewhat of a losing hazard, and required for successful achievement, not only memory and patience and linguistic accomplishments, but knowledge of ecclesiastical lore.

In theory these difficulties may appear formidable, but in practice they were non-important, owing to the fact that nothing that you ever wanted was ever contained in any of the shops, and, on the whole, it saved time and other things, to assume — with polite euphemism — that "to-day the shops were shut."

As time wore on a few more shops were opened, and a few commodities such as sugar—though not necessarily for public sale—put in an appearance. One day Pencka, one of our girl interpreters, came in with the good news that in one of the shops there was now a little sugar! Should we like some jam to be made? There was no fruit, either fresh or dried, but one of the shopkeepers had some dried rose leaves, and he would make us some jam out of these. And this romantic and excellent preserve was, for the short time that it lasted, a most welcome substitute for beef-dripping on brown bread.

CHAPTER XVI

It would no doubt have been better for the peace of mind of our staff if we could have adopted the same euphemistic attitude towards the Post Office that we adopted towards the shops, and have assumed that *it* too was permanently closed. I was personally not much worried, as I had arranged to have no letters forwarded from home. I could not in any case have deserted my work, and I did not want to be enervated by external worries. But those who were expecting to hear from home two or three times a week, and who knew that letters and parcels were being regularly dispatched, were naturally at first each day full of expectation. If there *was* a post office in working order, the hope that letters might be received was reasonable, until you had peeped behind the scenes. And then the wonder was that anything should ever be received at all. There was no *delivery* of letters. You were supposed to call for the post. The office was a good building which had been used—till the Bulgarian occupation of Kirk-Kilisse—as post office by the Turks. The débris of the old Turkish office—torn-up postal-orders, letters of credit, old account books—still littered the street and pavement just outside—ankle deep. Inside, a bran new Bulgarian post-office staff was in charge. Their procedure was as follows. During the few hours of the postal working day a certain number—very limited number—of mail bags would be dealt with, and if you were fortunate enough to enter the post office at a moment when a bag containing letters for yourself was being sorted, you stood a chance of being able, if you were agile, to snatch them and make off with them. But the sorters were new to their job, and in some cases could only read the Bulgarian Cyrillic characters. Letters addressed, therefore, in the old fashioned Latin type, stood small chance of being recognised and identified. But as it was further impossible, within the few working hours available each day (9 to 12 and 2 to 6), to deal with all the bags and arrears of bags that arrived in a single day, the sorters had an ingenious method of treatment. They would sort as many letters from as many bags as they could get through without worrying themselves, and then if a post bag was not emptied when closing time came, so much the worse for that post bag. It had lost its chance and was thenceforth banished to a dark and uninhabited back room. A new day dealt with new bags, and a sportive element of chance thus enveloped all communication from the outer world. Sometimes, however—and these were gala days—J., who was post-courier and treasurer to the Corps, would be allowed to have a sacred half-hour amongst the dead in that abandoned back room, and from amongst the masses of literary débris which strewed the floor would extract epistolary trophies of ancient date from the old country and emerge triumphant.

Outgoing letters and telegrams had, of course, to run the gauntlet of the censor. This meant sometimes hours of waiting in a long queue till it was your turn to present your letter and give details of the contents of the communication. Here also, ignorance on the part of some of the officials, of any language but the Bulgarian, had a restraining influence on the output. For the censor would only pass letters and telegrams that were written in a language which he could understand, and in a caligraphy which he could read. This latter condition

POST OFFICE IN KIRK-KILISSE.

irrevocably precluded me during my sojourn in the Balkans from communicating with my friends. *I* bore this with resignation, on the assumption that I could in emergency communicate with them by means of the non-committal telegram. But here again I was checkmated. For the postal authorities refused to send cables to countries of which they had never heard, and as the Bulgarian ignorance of general geography is almost as profound as the British ignorance of Balkan geography, my only method of communicating with, for instance, British Columbia and Nigeria was by cable via friends in London.

But even when letters did eventuate, the news contained in them seemed strangely insipid. Accounts of motor drives over flawless macadam roads! of dinner parties at which, as you knew, course after course of every delicacy in season or out of season would have been automatically handed round, and have been probably for the most part—horrible thought—as automatically refused! How dull seemed the alternative between champagne and claret, compared to the choice between water or no drink at all, or between impure water and nothing! And with this we were sometimes threatened. For our drinking water was obtained from a well in a house a few doors farther down the street, the water in the pumps in our own yards being obviously contaminated and unuseable for any purpose. But one evening the orderly, who had gone as usual to fetch water, did not return and there was no water to fill the kettles and the cooking pots. A hunt was instituted, and presently Kuko was found squatting composedly on the floor in one of the wards, warming his hands at the stove. An interpreter was fetched, and Kuko was asked why he had not done his duty and brought the water as usual to the kitchen? Did he not know that water was needed to cook the soldiers' dinner? He looked up in innocent surprise. "I could not bring water, the door was locked and there was no key. It was also sealed, but"—and he looked into the comforting stove again—"perhaps tomorrow the door will be open."

The door *was* open to-morrow, but it was not opened by warming our hands at the stove. The door did not open by itself. The history of the well and of the house and of its owner had immediately to be ascertained. It was found that the owner had for political reasons been expelled last night by the Government, who had then taken the keys and sealed the house. Our lieutenant had then to be dispatched, post haste, to the Commandant to ask for leave to have the keys in our own possession. This was eventually granted, but in the meantime a temporary water supply had to be discovered. We were fortunate in finding a well in another street not too far away, and this little difficulty vanished.

But in addition to superintendence of innumerable details and adjustment of minor difficulties such as this, it was necessary to be on the spot also to receive the various visitors —generals, medical directors, inspectors and officials of all kinds, who took the closest interest in our work. General Draganoff—the King's Chamberlain—honoured us on several occasions with a visit, and reported to King Ferdinand in flattering terms upon our improvized hospital. Madame Daneff, wife of the Minister who was subsequently delegate at the Peace Conference in London, also came to see us, and later, at Christmas time, gave us a welcome present of some bottles of wine.

Dr. Kiranoff, when he returned from Chatalja, was of course specially interested in coming often to witness, as he kindly put it, "the justification of his faith." He, together with his able and kindly assistant, Dr. Ivanoff, and our old friends the British and American and Italian Attachés, were often welcomed to our tea-table.

I am never likely to forget those teas. Amongst the many various duties which fell to my lot as Directrice of the Women's Convoy Corps Hospital at Kirk-Kilisse, I found none so difficult to manipulate, in accordance with any standard of success, as those five o'clock sit-down teas, with staff and visitors, in our mephitic little dining-room.

For the only chance of diverting the nostrils of our visitors from the pungent essence of cesspool with which our refectory was redolent, was to rivet the attention of the guests upon the conversation. But to maintain this at a sufficiently absorbing degree of brilliancy was not easy. With the exception of Col. Lyon— the British Attaché—who talked good French, English officers—you could take for granted— would speak no language but their own. Of the Bulgarian officers, some could speak, in addition to their own, only French, others only German, others again only Bulgarian, whilst an occasional Greek friend or a plenipotentiary from the Russian Hospital, would emit a hotch-potch of all the combined languages of Europe. And it was a juggler's feat to keep these different language balls all flying at once! If one ball dropped—sniff, sniff all round the table would, I knew, be chorused by inquisitive noses, which unfortunately all *sniffed* in Esperanto. I was thankful, after the armistice had been declared, and the scrimmage of out-patients awaiting in the hall their turn for treatment in the surgery was less, when we were able to abandon our horrid little stink-hole and take our meals in the screened-off portion of the entrance hall.

CHAPTER XVII

SURMISES, amongst visitors who had not previously known us, as to who and what the Convoy Corps are in England, were often quite interesting as a revelation of the knowledge possessed, on the Continent, of English societies. One day, for instance, we were honoured by a visit from the lady who was superintendent of the wards of one of the foreign Red Cross missions in Kirk-Kilisse; for foreign Red Cross missions other than the British had brought women nurses. She was a particularly well cultured woman, and spoke in excellent English. She introduced herself to me, and then said: "I am most in-te-rested in your or-ga-ni-zation, Madame Stobart,—you *are* ze Suffra-gettes—are you not?"

I was beginning to explain that we were not, when she interrupted apologetically. "Ah! no—no—How I am stupide! *I* know! Of course—you are ze *Salvation Army*!" The Suffragettes and the Salvation Army, the only two societies in England yet recognized on the Continent of Europe? Brass bands and advertisement not without results!

Another of our visitors was the cheery old Bishop of Stara Zagora. He came with an attendant priest and brought for the soldiers a most welcome gift of cigarettes. Up till that time it had been impossible to procure tobacco, and the patients had been clamouring for a smoke. He also brought for us women, not scent or sweetmeats, but a gift of extra good tobacco for cigarettes and some good old Madeira-like wine.

Our wounded had not before been visited by clergy. I had made inquiries and found that it was not desired by the soldiers. They would, I was told, have thought it was the signal of immediate death for all, had a priest appeared in the wards The Bishop merely walked through the wards distributing the cigarettes and an occasional blessing, as he passed from bed to bed. Nothing in the nature of a prayer was offered. He was a cheery old fellow and, full of pluck, was on his way to visit the cholera camp at Chatalja. Our hospital kept mercifully free from cholera, though patients might of course have been infected before entrance to our wards, and sixteen patients died from cholera in the infectious hospital in the street next to us. We were not supposed to take infectious cases, but after the armistice had been declared and no more fighting was taking place, medical cases became more frequent and needed careful watching, not only for cholera, but also for typhoid and a so-called malarial fever, both epidemic. The authorities had, however, early taken precautions against an outbreak of cholera. I had been summoned to a conference of the Heads of Hospitals three days after our arrival in Kirk-Kilisse, and precautionary measures were then discussed and subsequently put in force. The conference was held in the offices of the Commission Sanitaire. The President was Dr. Romanoff, and the practical director Professor Krauss. The room was, as usual, much overheated by one of those unmanageable stoves, which either emit too much heat and suffocate you, or, if checked, sulk and go out altogether, leaving you to an arctic temperature. I was more than ever convinced at this conference that the site of the Tower of Babel had been in Thrace, for the Babellian game was in full swing. The foreign missions in Kirk-Kilisse were represented, and everybody talked at once, in every conceivable

THE BISHOP OF STARA ZAGORA, AN ATTENDANT PRIEST, AND ONE OF OUR ENGLISH INTERPRETERS.

language. This might have been all very well if everybody had *understood* every language, but as the majority could speak one language only, and that imperfectly, it was marvellous how any business was transacted.

I reflected on the incongruity of the spectacle. Twentieth-century human beings—denizens of a much vaunted civilization, met together to discuss problems of life and death—unable to communicate their thoughts! If half the money that has been spent by man, in devising materials for the *destruction* of man, had been expended in devising means for verbal intercourse between man and man, the desire for mutual destruction would probably have vanished long ago. Has not the Tower of Babel period—of confusion in language and ideas—lasted long enough? When will come the Pentecost?

Our hospital visitors were always much interested in noting the cleanliness of the wards. For this was, as they knew, a result not too easily achieved. Improvized spittoons in the shape of open saucers made of red pottery, loomed largely, but the patients had a playful habit of throwing bones and scraps of food on the floor at meal times, and cleanliness was only attained by night-and-day efforts.

But in their persons the Bulgarian soldiers were extraordinarily cleanly. Their first craving on admission to hospital was always to be washed,—specially to have their feet washed. If for any reason the every morning routine all-over wash was delayed, even for a quarter of an hour, it was a grievance. When they were convalescent enough to be able to wash themselves, this was an operation which they thoroughly enjoyed. The condition of cleanliness in which they arrived, notwithstanding all they had endured, was marvellous, and I am always a disappointment to friends who desire to hear titillating stories of animal life in the Balkans.

Much interest was taken by our visitors in the theatre, for with the exception of the surgical instruments which had been brought from London, everything was improvized and homemade, with results that were astonishing. Visitors were surprised to find that the soldiers had no objections to operations being performed by women. I soon learned enough of the Bulgarian language to be able to understand the questions that were asked upon such points by visitors to the patients in the wards. The answers made always satisfied, and I think often surprised, the inquisitors. For the men with one accord agreed that they had never been so gently or so successfully handled by either doctors or nurses; whilst our own doctors and nurses corroborated, to their last day in hospital, the impression gained on the first night, that in qualities of courtesy, respect, and gratitude, no patients could surpass these Bulgarian peasant soldiers.

CHAPTER XVIII

BUT the patients were not only grateful to their doctors and nurses. They were also particularly appreciative of the efforts of those who catered for their gastronomic requirements. And the kitchen work, under Mrs. Godfray's charge, was by no means the least laborious nor the least trying to the temper. The kitchen contained no stove, and no cooking apparatus except a large open chimney-place. The only pots and pans, or culinary utensils, were three enormous stew-pots which Dr. Radeff had lent us from the Red Cross store at Sofia. We could requisition, through our lieutenant, certain quantities of brown bread, sugar, cheese, salt, tea and meat for the use of our patients and of ourselves. But "meat" did not mean convenient butcher-meat joints—or legs of mutton, or rolled ribs of beef—brought into the kitchen ready for cooking. "Meat" meant bullocks and sheep which arrived at the hospital door—not alive—but *whole*, and had to be cut up and transformed, from ram to mutton-broth, from trek-ox to tit-bit, by the three lady cooks. Every day during the seven weeks that we were in hospital, these three patient and untiring women prepared and cooked and served, under conditions of peculiar difficulty, all the meals for approximately 110 people every day; and, it must be added, to the entire satisfaction of the patients, who continually sent complimentary messages to the kitchen. It was soon discovered that good cooking meant, in their estimation, plenty of red pepper. Much variety was impossible, and the stock dish was a stew composed of chunks of beef or mutton, with gravy, rice, and as many vegetables as could be mustered. And if this was smothered, till it was the colour of terracotta, with pepper derived from the indigenous vegetable inappropriately called Chili, no dish from a Savoy restaurant menu could have given greater satisfaction.

The first meal for the patients on full diet was at 6 a.m., and consisted of tea, no milk, but plenty of sugar, half a loaf of brown bread for each man and a lump of cheese. Next followed the night nurses' breakfast at 6.30. Breakfast for the day nurses and the general staff was at 7. Brown bread and beef-dripping (tinned), tea and no milk, were the staple excitements of this repast. Occasionally, however, we were pampered with porridge, and still more rarely with eggs, which were sometimes brought in from country districts after the armistice began.

The men's second meal—dinner—the meal of the day, was at 12. It consisted of the much loved stew—as much as they could eat —and half a loaf of bread each man. Our own dinner at 1.30 was varied as much or as little as circumstances would permit. At 6 p.m. tea, bread and cheese again for the men, and at 7.30 followed our own supper of bully beef and cheese, brown bread and tea, or sometimes soup. Patients on special diet were given soup and arrowroot, but milk was for a long time unprocurable, and was only eventually to be had in very small quantities for the worst cases.

The superintendence of the serving of the men's meals was the most pleasurable duty of the day, for it gave opportunities of having a talk with the patients at a time when they would not be either under the nurse's or the doctor's ministrations. This dinner-hour was, for the cooks of course, the busiest of the day. The stew was emptied by the cook-in-chief into large enamel washing basins, and was then carried, with half loaves of bread, into the

HOSPITAL KITCHEN STAFF.
Cook-in-Chief abou to tackle a sheep.

different wards of all the three houses by the nurses, orderlies and interpreters. In each ward the stew was served by the nurses, and distributed to the patients by the orderlies and also by the interpreters, who all did fine service in any work that was required in either wards, theatre, kitchen or surgery, wherever they were at the moment needed.

And they were much needed everywhere, for of our small staff, a proportion, those on night duty, were of course by day absent for sleep and rest. Some again were on the sick list, and we were as a rule left with none too many for the daily task.

Of our young men interpreters, one was, in normal times, in charge of the orphanage maintained by Mr. Mahoney, in Sofia, for Macedonian and Thracian peasant boys. He lid excellent work for us. Another, a splendidly serviceable and resourceful lad, was the son of an English merchant at Jamboli. He was a fine type of an English boy. He never took "no" for an answer if we wanted "yes," and he was invaluable to us.

The two Bulgarian boys had been brought up and educated by Mr. Mahoney at the orphanage, and also in England and Ireland. They both had family histories which were painfully typical of Turkish suzerainty. One of them told us he remembered when he was a child, that he was one day sitting drinking coffee in his home, with his father and mother, when suddenly some Turks burst into the room, and for no conceivable reason began violently to beat his father about the head with big sticks. His mother had then snatched him—the boy—in her arms and fled. She was warned not to return, but after three months she could not resist going back to the old home to see what had been left. She found in the living room—which was otherwise as she had left it—her husband's skull and the palm of one hand upon the floor.

The other Bulgarian boy came to me a few days before we closed the hospital, and asked if I could very kindly dispense with his further services and give him leave to go to visit his home. His father had been a priest in the Thracian village in which he and his family lived, but, suspected by the Turks of preaching treason, had been sent for three years to prison and had there died. And now, the boy told me, that shortly after this war had broken out, the Turks had slaughtered 300 out of the 600 inhabitants of his village, and he was now anxious to get back and see if his mother and sisters were still living, or if they were perchance amongst the massacred. I asked him with surprise why he had not applied earlier for leave to go? I could not imagine how he could, all this time, have endured the suspense of not knowing whether the only relatives he had on earth were alive or dead. He replied calmly: "If they are dead, they are dead and I cannot bring them back. I could not leave you here whilst there was work for our wounded to be done. But now, perhaps, I can be spared?"

And this spirit of philosophy, of patriotism and also of chivalrous courtesy, was typical of the Bulgarian nation. I had been prepared for the possibility of annoyance from the curiosity of men visitors who in a Turkish environment would be unaccustomed to seeing such work conducted solely by women—by women who, absorbed in their work, would have no time for sex frivolities. But Bulgarian men of all classes could give lessons to the men of most nations of Europe in their attitude towards women, and the only levity I encountered from the first day to the last of our undertaking was from a German officer. He was one day hanging around outside the hospital door, and I asked him if he wished to see over the hospital.

In reply he asked me with a smile of amusement—who we were. I was explaining to him that we were an organization of English women, when he interrupted with the tell-tale question, "Sind sie alle hübsch?" He had given himself away, and I replied promptly, "No—nothing of that sort, they're all over fifty. Would you care to see over the hospital now?"

And the young man turned away sorrowfully,—he had many engagements.

CHAPTER XIX

But a visitor who did eventuate, and to some purpose, was General Vazoff, lately appointed Governor-General of Lozengrad. He went over the hospital, and, highly appreciative, asked me if I would pay him a return call at his headquarters in the town, and tell him more about our work, as he wished to write a report to send to the King's Secretary. I therefore went one afternoon—accompanied by Dr. Kiranoff—and we had a long and interesting talk about many things. We discussed the terrible destitution prevailing amongst the peasantry as a result of the war, and General Vazoff said, " Yes, it was bad enough now, but when the war was over, the need for relief would be even greater. Whilst fighting continued, those who had been driven from their homes were sheltering as best they could—anywhere, but when the war was finished, and families were re-united and went back to their old villages to start their normal life again, money would be needed to rebuild their houses, buy their seeds, and stock their farms." That, he said, would be the time when relief would be most needed and when, as we all agreed, it would be most difficult to obtain, because public attention in England and elsewhere would by then have transferred itself to some more topical drama of sensation. And that, as I also realized, would be the time when the steadfastness of Noel Buxton and his Balkan Committee would prove their value.

We then discussed the hospital of the Convoy Corps, and General Vazoff, much interested, inquired the conditions under which we had come to Bulgaria to nurse their wounded. Had we come under the auspices of the British Red Cross? At this point Dr. Kiranoff, to my surprise and consternation, broke in with some vehemence and gave me away. The B.R.C.S., he said, "sent only *men* with their missions to Bulgaria to nurse the sick and wounded. They did not think the conditions in Bulgaria would be suitable for women. Madame Stobart," he said, "thought the Red Cross Society were mistaken and came out on her own."

"Bravo, bravo,—that was well done, and we are very grateful," enthusiastically exclaimed

General Vazoff—to my great surprise, for I had been taken aback at Dr. Kiranoff's frankness, thinking that my lawlessness would probably be disapproved by the General. But it was otherwise.

"I wish," the former added, after some further remarks, as he glanced round the sparsely furnished room which was serving as his office—"I could give you some souvenir. Ah!" he exclaimed, as his eye fell on an oil painting, mounted but unframed, standing on a table against the wall. He went up to the picture. "Look," he said, as he took it in his hands and came towards me—"this is absolutely the only possession I have here. It is a picture of a typical Turkish country house on the Maritza. I looted it a few days ago. Will you accept it—as an insignificant token of appreciation and gratitude?" I of course accepted the picture with pride. To me it was not insignificant, for was it not a testimony of the recognition by the highest Bulgarian officials, of the value of the work accomplished by the Convoy Corps?

Dr. Kiranoff then left, and I was also preparing to march off with my loot, when the General rang a little hand-bell and told an orderly, who came in response, to order the carriage to come round at once, and then he insisted that I should allow him to take me for a drive and let him show me the environs of Kirk-Kilisse. Whilst the carriage was getting ready, the Governor wrote and gave me, two letters, one to the Queen and one to the Secretary of the King, giving an enthusiastic report of the work of the Convoy Corps. He told me I was to be sure and deliver these letters myself in person, and then the carriage was announced. The weather was cold, with frosts at night, and I had no overcoat with me. Noticing this, the General gallantly took off the beautiful grey-blue coat which he was wearing and enwrapped me. And as I remonstrated, he sent for another coat for himself, and then, clothed in the voluminous and gorgeous uniform of a Bulgarian general, I solemnly descended the stairs with the Governor, and, followed by the orderlies, was bowed into the open phaeton drawn by two horses which awaited us at the door. We drove through Kirk-Kilisse, receiving and returning the salutations of the people and of the soldiers, who as usual crowded the narrow streets, and out into the country beyond.

We passed, amongst the vineyards by the roadside, many groups of small oblong mounds of earth—the shallow resting-places of the gallant dead who had fallen in the fight around this town. It was fortunate that, as the Governor explained, the earth here possesses some curious chemical properties which seem to prevent the usual malodorous results of decomposition.

General Vazoff showed me, amongst other points of interest, the place where in a small village, now destroyed, a certain Turkish General had, a week or two before, stood and wept—for tears are not the monopoly of women—at the defeat which his army at Kirk-Kilisse had sustained.

But the battle of Kirk-Kilisse was decided not, as was recorded in the papers, in the streets of Kirk-Kilisse, there was no fighting in the town itself, but in the vineyards just outside, and in the trenches of Fort Bulgaria. The Bulgarians had come trooping down over the mountains and attacked the fort just before dark one evening. The Turks defended it till nightfall, but in the morning, when the Bulgarians expected to renew the fighting, they found to their surprise that the Turks had fled towards Adrianople, and Kirk-Kilisse was now theirs.

The dispositions of the respective armies had already been explained to me by a military officer who had been sent with a message for me from the Queen. He had one evening walked with some of us to the Fort—about two miles distant from Kirk-Kilisse, and shown us the trenches, now strewn with empty cartridge cases, from which the Turks had made their short defence, and it was therefore interesting now in my drive with the Governor to fill in the canvas and acquire an aeroplanic vision of the whole battle.

We drove and talked till it was dark, when the General invited me to take coffee with him in the town. But it was now time for the men's tea, which I never missed. The coachman therefore received the order in Bulgarian "á la mission des dames Anglaises," and I was deposited at the hospital, wondering, as I alighted and the Governor drove off saluting, if there really *were* people in the world who were bored with life?

SOME OF THE 140 GUNS AT KIRK-KILISSE
CAPTURED BY THE BULGARIANS.

CHAPTER XX

I SOON discovered three people who were on the verge of being *very* bored with life—these were our three washing girls, who were waiting to see me before they went home from work. I had found that with a crowded hospital it was impossible for our staff to spare time for washing all the soiled sheets, pillow-cases, night-garments, etc. of the patients, and I tried immediately we started hospital, to find washer-women—either Bulgarian or Turkish, to come every day. But apparently there were either no women in Kirk-Kilisse, or the job wasn't popular, and for several days I drew a blank, till finally I went as usual, as a last resource, to the Commandant, and he promised that bipeds of some sort should be sent to wash for us.

And the next morning, to my great joy, three strong, nice-looking girls put in an appearance at the hospital. I sent for one of our particularly intelligent girl interpreters to come and explain the nature of the work required. She talked for about five minutes, whilst I was busy attending to somebody else, and told the girls, in Bulgarian, all that would be expected of them, and then she turned to ask me some question about soap or washtub. I then noticed that upon the faces of the washing trio there still rested that same look of placid indifference which I had observed when they first came into the office. And they had neither of them opened their lips. I asked them in Bulgarian if they understood what had been explained to them. They shook their heads. Good gracious!—are they dumb?—I asked the interpreter. *She* then asked them if they had understood, and immediately the flood gates were opened, and a language, of which neither of us comprehended one word, was poured upon us, in triplicate. There was no doubt about the eloquence of the language. But I had no time for an eloquence which I didn't understand, so I said "Ja, ja—exactly so," and, smiling benignly, seized them all three by the arms, and dragged them to a shed in which were wooden trenches which had been made for washing-troughs by the old carpenters. I pointed to a pile of soiled linen on the floor, sent for water, put some soap into their hands and then, uttering a few guttural blessings, closed the door and left them. Conscious of the shortcomings of a somewhat scantily equipped laundry, I kept at a distance all the morning, but sent a messenger to bring back a report. Washing was apparently proceeding, but the messenger had not stopped to observe details; she had precipitately fled when, on opening the door to look in, she had been greeted by a broadside of gesticulative and unintelligible jargon. However, though the trio were particularly dense in understanding anything that tended to imply *work*, they had a wonderful knack of finding means of expression for anything they wanted for themselves. After a couple of hours of washing, they sauntered boldly arm-in-arm into my office, and with the forefingers of their right hands pointing at their widely open mouths, and their left hands placed pathetically over their little Marys,—left me no escape from the inference that they were hungry and that it was dinner-time for them.

I discovered before the day was over, from our lieutenant, whose mother was a Greek, that the girls were Grecian; but the language of signs was, I found, in many ways convenient and time-saving, and as we had no Greek interpreter, we availed ourselves of Hobson's choice and did excellently without, for the remainder of our time in hospital.

I often used to wish, as I looked out on all the linen hung up to dry on ropes slung across our tiny backyard, that the many well-intentioned folks, who in England had with much effort contributed bed garments for "the wounded in the Balkans," could have cast their eyes along that line before they had sat down to their sewing parties. They would have saved themselves much wasted labour. Many recipients of consignments of "clothes for the wounded," and also for "the destitute," were much embarrassed to know what to do with the bundles of unuseable rubbish with which they had been flooded.

We were fortunate in having been able to ascertain at Sofia the style of bed-garment approved by the Bulgarian soldier-peasantry, and had provided for their use, washing shirts in flannel and in linen, and linen bed-drawers —the latter specially arranged for the possibility of leg and thigh injuries. And these were all thoroughly appreciated by our patients. But some of the other missions, on the other hand, had much trouble on the score of bed garments. They had provided for their prospective patients, long flannel night-shirts of a pattern not even presented now upon the English stage, and the soldiers one and all had refused to wear what they considered an insufficient and indecent covering. They demanded to be put to bed in their dirty old uniforms rather than submit to the indecorum of a night-shirt.

And this, although apparently an insignificant trifle, was a matter of some concern, for of the injuries received by the soldiers in battle, the larger proportion were in the legs. I have no knowledge of the statistics of other hospitals, but in our fourteen wards—apart from the out-patients, of whom the larger proportion would naturally be suffering from hand and arm wounds—I one day estimated that of the eighty-four patients at that moment in the hospital, forty-eight had been hit in the legs and sixteen in the arms; and of the remainder, the injuries were distributed amongst heads, shoulders, ribs, back, etc., whilst seven of the cases were medical.

This prevalence of leg wounds was explained to me by the soldiers as due to the fact that the Turkish soldier is so illiterate that he cannot read the sighting on his rifle and aims point-blank, with the usual result that the bullet hits *below* the mark at which it is aimed. Even some of the Turkish officers—presumably some of those risen from the ranks, under the old régime—were also unable to read or write.

Shrapnel, Grenade, Mauser and Mannlicher bullets each told its own graphic tale. It was of interest to note that the Mauser, in general use by the Turks, was more merciful in effect than the Mannlicher used by the Bulgarian army. But of the murderous projectiles used, shrapnel was, of course, the most disastrous in its effects, and a terrible shattering was the result. In one case a large portion of the buttocks had been completely torn away, and it seemed impossible that the man should live, but he, like most of our patients, recovered in marvellous fashion. Another man came in with his right arm shockingly shattered by shrapnel. He had travelled in the usual comfortless ox-carts for five days, from Lule Burgas. He arrived in an exhausted condition, and was suffering as many were, when first admitted, from severe shock. He was discovered the next morning weeping disconsolately. We asked him what was the matter, and he then confided to us, after a little hesitation, that he was engaged to be married, and he was terribly afraid that if—as he feared

—he should lose his arm, his fiancée—who was, of course, the only girl in all the world—might refuse to marry him. At that time we also feared that his arm could not possibly be saved, but he was told that if he kept up his spirits and was brave, he had a good chance of getting well and keeping his arm. And, owing to the skill of the doctors and the devotion of the nurses, the arm was saved and our friend—a particularly handsome and attractive personality—will it is hoped by now be safely married, and in process of living happily ever after!

And now, as I am myself neither a doctor nor a nurse, and contributed therefore nothing whatever directly to the therapeutical results, it is, I hope, permissible here to dilate a little on the really wonderful percentage of recoveries effected by our doctors and our nurses. Amongst 729 cases that were treated, there was only one death, and that was a medical case. The patient, who was apparently recovering, and had that very afternoon been much aggrieved because he was not allowed to get up and dress, died suddenly and unexpectedly in the night, from heart trouble following, as the post-mortem confirmed, a mild and incipient attack of typhoid.

It is true—in mitigation of this somewhat remarkable record—that the men, who belonged to a vigorous healthy stock, had been accustomed all their lives to plain food and wholesome living and were free in an exceptional degree from immoral diseases, and were therefore peculiarly exempt from excesses of all kinds, and yielded the more readily to treatment. It is true also that many of these 729 patients were out-patients who would, of course, be comparatively less seriously wounded. But the nature of the injuries of those others—approximately 300, who filled the wards during the seven weeks of our residence, was severe enough to tax the ability and care of the ablest of both professions of doctors and of nurses. I attribute their success not only to the skill and restraint of the doctors in operations, and to the devotion of the nurses in the wards, but to the extreme care taken by the Sisters in the sterilization of the instruments, etc., in the theatre. Soldiers who came into the hospital with their brains protruding through their skulls, at first paralysed in speech and in every limb, men with buttocks shot away, men with arms and legs shattered —with wounds which made it impossible to believe, as you gazed upon them, that this

GROUP OF CONVALESCENT PATIENTS GOING HOME.
The two band boys in front are aged 14 and 15. Their brother was killed at Chatalja.

WAR AND WOMEN 169

raw, bleeding, nauseous-smelling object formed part of a human being,—these one and all recovered in what seemed to me miraculous fashion, and I am confident that I may, without partiality, justly praise the skill and devotion of the doctors and the nurses and the patience and the dogged hard work of the kitchen staff which effected this result.

It was to my mind also worthy of note that this little band of women—drawn from classes accustomed in their own homes to every luxury, should have withstood not only the work, but the hardships and privations, without a grumble or a word of discontent from the time they left Victoria Station to the time when they returned there in safety.

I must, however, also praise the character of the soldiers themselves. It would be difficult, I think, to find in any country a purer, more wholesome, chivalrous type of men than those whom it was our privilege to heal. The majority—80 per cent.—of these peasant soldiers were, as I ascertained in each case from personal inquiry, proprietors of their own land, owning on an average from 10 to 200 dekkars—from two, that is, to fifty acres. It was not therefore perhaps surprising that an army composed of soldiers of this type, should have been, in their war with the allies, victorious against the Turk. No better argument against a professional as compared with a "territorial" army could well, it seemed to me, have been afforded than by this war in which by far the larger amount of professionalism was on the losing side. If wars were only fought by those who, like the Bulgarian peasants, had everything to lose and nothing personally to gain by going to war, there would be fewer wars, and those only would be fought which had moral justice rather than political expediency as the compelling force.

In her subsequent war against her former allies Bulgaria has laid herself open to a charge of greed and land-hunger. It is possible that—once in the field and grown accustomed to the horrors of war, faced too with the prospect of destitution which in any event probably awaited them on their return to their homes when the war was over—the Bulgarian army may have succumbed to the human passion of territorial greed and aggrandizement. If that were so, they have paid the penalty. But no one who had mixed and spoken, as I did, for weeks with hundreds of these Bulgarian soldiers and their officers, would for a moment believe that the prospect of a problematic extension of boundaries would in the first onset have persuaded these 300,000 peasants to leave their homes and families, to abandon their crops and means of livelihood, to risk death and mutilation for themselves and destitution for their wives and children, and to come out on the battlefield against an army of professional and life-long soldiers. The Bulgarian peasant, though he has proved himself to be a soldier equal to Europe's best, did not fight from a passion of land-hunger nor for the love of fighting. He was driven from his homestead by an *Ideal*, he was sustained in the dismal trenches by an *Ideal*, and the point of his bayonet was sharpened by an *Ideal*. The Ideal that drove those many thousand peasants who filled the Bulgarian hospitals, from the lethargy of their agricultural life and the peacefulness of their domestic happiness, was the Ideal of *Nationhood*, intuitive in all those who have an evolutionary mission to perform. The first stage of progress towards nationhood is Freedom—and Freedom was impossible under the heel of the Turk. Therefore the Turk must go. This—the Ideal which inspired the Bulgars in their crusade against the Turks, will remain as their Ideal till it is accomplished. Europe may, as far as Bulgaria is concerned.

believe what she likes as to the greed and rapacity of the Bulgarian people. Europe will make a great mistake if she thinks these people will ever abandon an Ideal which they have once visualized. The Turk, they said, must go, and the Turk was defeated, not because he has no good qualities,—he probably has as many potential virtues as the Bulgars or even as the British nation. The Turk was defeated, when the odds were not overwhelmingly against him, because he has no longer an Ideal. His old Ideal—the Mahommedan faith—was not built upon the Rock of Ages, but upon the sands of Time, and is being annihilated by the tide of progress.

The history of all dynamic movements is universally the same. They must either expand and grow with the growing life around them, or become fossils, fit only for museums. The spirit of cruelty, of intolerance, of sensuality that breathes in every sentence of the Koran, is not capable of adaptation to new conditions. The Koran was a creed of opportunism. The inspiration was spurious—the fire is burnt out.

The young Turk had become aware that the core of his faith was rotten, that the inspiration of his religion was dead, that he had no longer a religious Ideal. Pathetically in his need he had turned—blindly—for inspiration, to that Paris which had supplied him in this world with the joys which his religion had only promised in the next. He sought, in the cold and barren Positivism of Comte, for that religious zeal, fervour and idealism which alone can drive nations on to victory. He sought life's blood from a stone—the result was disaster and defeat.

In that Turkish army of professional soldiers there was lacking that psychical "something more" which on the Bulgarian side converted hordes of imperfectly trained peasants into an army which has proved itself worthy—with some mistakes excepted—to rank amongst the finest Europe has known. I disbelieve the stories that have been circulated by their enemies, of atrocities committed by these Bulgarian peasant soldiers. They are a proud and reserved race, and would no more think of elaborately defending themselves against the falsehoods uttered by their enemies, than they would themselves utter falsehoods against those enemies. But if, when every man's hand was against them, and after months of fighting, during which their eyes had rested on nothing but blood and carnage,—if then the power of suggestion produced its accustomed result, and gentle-men like those we nursed in our hospital at Kirk-Kilisse, have at times seen red—that would not be an argument against the humanity of the Bulgarian soldier, it would be an indictment against the barbarity of a "Civilized Europe" which still elaborately trains its populations to settle their differences and adjust their boundaries by *blood and carnage.*

The barbarism of "taking life" lies not in the Jesuitical distinction between taking life in cold blood or taking life in the heat of battle. It is the "taking life" that is the barbarism.

But Mahommedanism—the religion invented by a man for the benefit of men only, still absorbs the religious devotion of one-fifth of the human race. Is it then a wonder that the world's Ideals of humanity and of heroism should be tinctured by essence of maleness?

Men are said to love danger better than work. *If* this is a fact, would not this insensibly tend to blur their distinction between Ideals of humaneness and of heroism?

It may be true, "as saith Zarathustra," that "only where there are graves are there resurrections." But is it not also a truth, not unknown to history, that resurrections are sometimes revealed first to women?

May it not possibly be from women that the world will eventually learn to realize that "God rules the universe," as Fourier reminds us, "by attraction, not by force"?

CHAPTER XXI

BUT the world will never learn anything from women who only acquire knowledge at second hand. Argument from intellect alone is powerless to persuade mankind to *action*. Intellect is only an accessory of human nature, and is therefore unconvincing to the *hearts* of the multitude. Whole libraries of learned treatises on the Peace Movement, which might have interested my intellect, would never have moved the "real me" as this was moved by *feeling* the tragedies that I saw enacted everywhere in that Balkan charnel-house. The B.R.C.S., in sending out units of men only to nurse the sick and wounded in Bulgaria, acted doubtless with the best intentions. But they acted according to the lights of half a century ago. The purblind policy of shielding women against their will from a knowledge of truths, however unpleasant these may be, is disastrous not only for women, but for the community at large. The B.R.C. unit, which established a hospital in the old Turkish Barracks, two miles outside Kirk-Kilisse, performed an excellent service, and Major Birrell, R.A.M.C., who was in charge, and Major Hudson and Captain Byam, deserve the greatest credit for their success in carrying out a horribly difficult job. They had, I believe, been dispatched as a unit for a *field* hospital, and had to transmogrify themselves into a base hospital unit as best they could. They made bricks without straw as British officers can. But if the women of the Convoy Corps had not, by an odd coincidence, been close at hand, working on parallel lines and giving testimony of British *women's* goodwill to work apart from all pusillanimous possibilities, wherever work was needed,—the exclusive maleness of the Red Cross unit in the Turkish Barracks would have been a standing humiliation to Great Britain.

For this Red Cross unit of *men only* signified that a prominent organization in Great Britain is still breathing the atmosphere of the times of our great-grandmothers, and fails to realize that women can no longer be content to float idly upon the surface, but feel it their duty, at whatever cost to themselves, to plumb the depths of life.

For the first three weeks that we were in Kirk-Kilisse we saw nothing of the men's unit, which had arrived shortly before us. But eventually—perhaps when rumours of our self-containedness and of the not unsuccessful nature of our work had penetrated to those Turkish Barracks—the officers called upon us. They were then very friendly, and we became much indebted to their kindness in lending us from time to time their X-ray apparatus for the location of bullets. They were, on their first visit to us, probably as curious to see how a hospital could be run by women without any men, as I was to know how a hospital could possibly be run by men without any women. As I was showing them round the wards in which our women were all busily attending to the patients, I suggested laughingly, wasn't it very brave of the men to attempt to run a hospital without women? "I can't believe," I added, daringly, "that your men could, for instance, be as scrupulous with the sterilization of the instruments in the theatre as the women, or that they would understand so well how to keep their wards clean, or that they would be so patient or so careful in the nursing, or——"

"Ah!" interrupted one of the officers, "if

you would exchange some of your women for some of our men, we'd bless you to all eternity!"

But that exchange was not effected.

Later, however, as Xmas drew near, and the stress of work in both hospitals had grown considerably less, owing to the continuance of the armistice, they very kindly asked us if we would care to join forces with them for dinner on Xmas Day. We could legitimately by then allow our respective staffs a couple of hours relaxation. And we accepted the proposal with gladness.

The Commandant, to whom the scheme was confided, then very kindly put an automobile at the disposal of the two hospitals, and told us we could drive out to any of the outlying villages, where, away from the main route of the army, poultry, etc., might still be left, and requisition, for payment, any turkeys, chickens, geese, or sucking pigs that we could find.

One morning, therefore, two of the Red Cross officers and one of their interpreters (an American missionary who worked in Sofia) called for me in the automobile, and we dashed off on what journalistic headlines might not inaptly have called "A British raid upon Turkey."

Farmyards in Thrace were, we found,

sensibly conducted. Pigs were all born grown-up, for there was not—I was thankful to find—a sucking pig in the whole country. And no one at all was born a goose, for there were also none of these to be found. There was, however, as might be expected, a turkey in most places.

Our tactics on arriving in a village were as follows. First we would go to the house of the Commandant, and arouse him from either his morning, his midday, his afternoon, or his evening slumber, and obtain from him permission to commandeer whatever animal we should covet. Next we sallied forth on foot into the village, and, making for greens, open spaces and farmyards, we would mark down any winged animals we saw. So far so good. But the business of tracking the *owners* of the winged animals was another proposition. The poultry apparently had no owners—belonged to a republic of their own, for no bird that we ever selected ever belonged to anybody. Or—the owner was "at the front," and in his absence no one had authority to sell. Even if, eventually, by Jesuitry and cross-examination, an owner *was* run to earth, he was always "a stranger to the place"—"knew nothing about any turkeys or to whom they belonged," and then—*in extremis*—he would finally protest that he loved his turkeys and wouldn't part from them, as he had no use for money. We guessed this meant that, guided by past experience during the war, he had no faith that he would ever see the money if he parted from his birds, so our next move was to jingle money in our hands ostentatiously. Then we would stroll casually towards the little café, and invite our friend to come in with us and sit down and drink a glass of Masticha and a cup of coffee—coffee which must now be called not " café Turque," but " café Balkanique." During this process the ramparts generally fell, but in the last resort we would threaten to take the business into our own hands, and choose and kill and make off with what birds we liked. And immediately the look of detached unconcern on the face of our old ruffian would give place to one of interest, and the conversion of the owner into a willing seller was accomplished.

All we had then to do was to persuade him, for his own good, that a huge piece of fortune had come his way with our entrance into his village, and that five francs in his pocket was of considerably more value to him than a tough old turkey-cock strutting aimlessly about on the road outside ; and then, after perhaps another glass of Masticha, the bargain would be struck, and our only remaining job would be to catch our birds, a performance needing some athleticism.

We collected altogether that day eighteen turkeys and twenty-six chickens, and we had a fine business tying them—all-alive-oh! and as obstreperous as their former owners—to the top of the car.

But before we left the last village the news had leaked out that we came from hospitals, and that the two khaki-clad officers were doctors. Immediately we were besieged with requests for medicines, and the maimed, the halt and the blind were brought to us in expectation of immediate cure.

For here again the results of warfare were cruelly apparent. Almost without exception every child in the village was suffering from complaints which were the effect of lack of nourishment. The breadwinners had been on the field of battle for four months, and any stock, such as sheep and goats, if formerly possessed, had long ago been sold. Even flour to make the ubiquitous brown bread was hard to get.

A more pitiably anæmic-looking village-full of women and children, it would be difficult to find.

One pale-faced, handsome woman was in great distress, and implored us to come to her

Interpreter persuading Peasant that Five Francs in the Pocket is worth more than a Turkey-cock on the Green.

house and see her little son. He had been lying ill for two weeks, and she could do nothing for him. We went back with her to her one-roomed hut. The little fellow, about three years old, was lying in high fever on a mat—the usual bed—upon the floor, with a covering of blankets. He was white and emaciated, had a hard hacking cough and frequent bleedings of the nose. With the usual ignorance of peasants, the mother had been trying to make him eat the hard brown bread, and was distressed because he could not swallow it. My two doctor friends told her she must procure milk and give him beaten-up eggs, for she kept a few fowls, and send in to the hospital for some medicine next day. They then went outside and administered advice and treatment to a group of women and children and old folks who had collected with a wonderful assortment of ailments. For, warned by a previous experience, my friends had brought a medicine chest. I was then requested by the mother of the little boy to squat indoors, Turkish style, on a mat on the floor, and talk to her.

She fixed her dark eyes, full of fear, searchingly upon me. "Will he die?" she asked. "If—if he were not—here—when—when his father comes back from the war——!"

"But of course he will be here—if you do as the doctors tell you," I answered. "But it all depends on you. Keep this kettle going"—we had rigged up a bronchitis kettle on the open fireplace—"and give him milk and eggs and the medicine which will be fetched to-morrow, and he'll soon be well."

She was comforted, and then she turned her attention to me. I had to explain every item of my uniform—where I was working and why I had come so far to help her people, and—then suddenly again, "Oh! but you're *sure* he won't die?" And I was glad when the doctors came inside, as it was now dark, to examine by a small oil wick, the only available light, the eyes of an old man—this woman's father. He had cataract, and was told he must go to Kirk-Kilisse to a hospital and have it removed.

It was then time for us to go, and as we said good-bye, the mother pressed into my hands a basket of fresh eggs. "Backsheesh," she whispered, and as I of course refused to accept it· "Yes, yes, you must take them," she added surprised, unable to understand that the doctors could have performed a service for nothing, and that we could deliberately refuse an offer of six good eggs! We could only make her desist by reminding her that the boy needed all the eggs she would be able to give him.

If we had not all been fully occupied in our own wards, there was plenty of work to do in doctoring the non-combatants in the outlying villages, where medical advice was of course out of the question. But we returned with our turkey-laden car to the routine work at our respective hospitals, having agreed that our combined staffs should meet on Xmas Day at a restaurant in Kirk-Kilisse, where we should neither of us have to be ourselves responsible for the cooking, and eat our Xmas dinner in comparative luxury.

The Bulgarian Xmas is, like the Greek and Russian festival, celebrated thirteen days later than that of the Anglican Church, and our patients all grew very excited when they heard that we were going to have a " Kissi-mas " of our own.

Early on Xmas morning, when I went as usual round the wards, I felt the atmosphere was full of a suppressed excitement, and before I could pronounce my usual greeting " Kak ste? "—How are you?—there was a general rustling of sheets, and the patients, all sitting up in bed, craning forward their necks, shouted triumphantly with one accord, " Melly Kissi-mas."

This they had been taught by our energetic and invaluable girl-interpreters, Pencka and Adriana, and the night nurses told me that many of the soldiers had spent the night muttering the words over and over again, in their anxiety not to forget them when the fateful moment arrived. The relief at having now safely disgorged these verbal calibans was obviously intense.

No English Church services had hitherto been available for our staff, who had contented themselves on Sundays with attending the Bulgarian service held in one of the Greek churches. But on this Xmas morning a service, to which we were invited, was conducted in the Turkish Barracks by the Red Cross Unit's American missionary interpreter. This gave a realistic touch of Xmas to the day.

A portion of both hospital staffs was of course obliged to be absent from the Xmas evening dinner, and remain on duty with the patients; but the remainder, about forty of us, enjoyed at 7 p.m. a truly memorable feast. For the restaurant keeper had played up well, and had kindly kept the room all day for our exclusive use, in order that we might decorate it with boughs of mistletoe, with which the trees around Kirk-Kilisse abounded. We had also,

A Satisfactory Bargain over Turkey.

for the occasion, taken down our Union Jack, Red Cross and Bulgarian flags, which were suspended on a rope across the road between the two main houses of our hospital, and with these, together with the flags belonging to our friends of the Red Cross unit, the room looked appropriately festive and British-Bulgarian.

After many weeks of trek ox and of stew-pot food, those turkeys took on an ambrosial flavour which no English turkey could have rivalled, and the tinned plum puddings sent out by our friends from the old country were universally declared to be "the best we had ever eaten."

The restaurant keeper had been duly coached to send the pudding in "on fire," but when the time came, the tidings circulated that "Bulgarian brandy would not light." We couldn't of course believe this, and thought it might be a superstition on the part of our landlord. But the united efforts of ourselves and our Red Cross messmates definitely failed to ignite that stolid Bulgarian brandy.

"Our brandy is meant for drink, not for fireworks," explained our host as he disdainfully watched our efforts. These were grotesquely futile till the brilliant suggestion was made, that a little *English* brandy—of which there was some in a flask—might set off the

Bulgarian spirit. The result was instantaneous, and the puddings made their entrance in orthodox fashion, surrounded by tongues of fiery flame.

Thus not only our Bulgarian patients, but even the Bulgarian brandy, chivalrously acknowledged that a little English help was good for the spirits! This impromptu, interlarded in my toast to the Bulgarian King and Queen, much pleased our Bulgarian interpreters. Toasts and speeches were beautifully short, by agreement, but could not on such an occasion be utterly omitted.

Major Birrell proposed our King and Queen and sang the praises of the Convoy Corps, whilst I toasted the Bulgarian King and Queen and spoke words of appreciation of the friendliness of the Red Cross unit toward us. I had the pleasure also of reading aloud a telegram which I had just received from Queen Eleonora wishing the Women's Convoy Corps a happy Xmas.

Then after the singing of "Auld lang syne," the Bulgarian national "Shumi Maritza" and "God save the King," we all dispersed and hurried back through the dark muddy streets to our patients, some of us not unthankful that a day always full of painful memories had come to a successful close.

CHAPTER XXII

Now that the armistice had been in progress for three weeks, and the authorities were all of opinion that the war was over, and that hostilities were not likely to be renewed, the question of closing the hospital and returning home had to be considered. Other foreign missions had already either left or were about to leave. We had for some time had no fresh *surgical*, only medical cases, and if we were to remain longer, our hospital must be converted into a medical hospital for typhoids and other fever patients. And though we were prepared to take anything that came along, amongst the surgical cases, whilst conditions of war prevailed, our position in the middle of the town, and our lack of sanitary requirements, would not, I con-considered, justify our filling the hospital with typhoids and infectious cases which need sanitary precautions we were unable to provide. A serious epidemic amongst patients as well as nurses might have resulted. Some of our staff, which was already small enough, could not in any case have remained for a fresh term of work. Major Birrell also considered the time ripe for the departure of his unit, and as he and I had consulted together and had decided to act simultaneously in the matter of closing our hospitals, we together visited Dr. Kiranoff. He much regretted our departure, but he agreed that the surroundings of the Convoy Corps Hospital were unsuitable for fever patients, and he arranged to take over our remaining serious cases and combine them with those of the Red Cross unit in the Turkish Barracks, under the charge of Bulgarian doctors.

Subsequently our own three doctors decided to remain in Kirk-Kilisse and assist the Bulgarian Red Cross authorities; and later, when the British Red Cross unit had departed, were transferred to the Turkish Barracks, where, as I hear, and can well believe, they have rendered excellent service.

We foresaw that the news of our prospective departure would not be welcome to those of our patients who would not be well enough to return to their homes or to their regiments, but would have to be transferred to another hospital. We decided, therefore, to keep them in ignorance as long as possible.

But the news leaked out, and one morning, when at 6.30 I was as usual making my round of the hospital, I found one of the patients in the first ward I visited, with the tears streaming down his cheeks. We always called this man Dobrai—which means "Very well"—because though he was seriously ill with a complicated fracture of the femur, due to shrapnel-shattering, he always replied "Dobrai, dobrai" when we asked him how he felt, just as a reassurance to us that our treatment was successful.

I was, of course, horrified to find our much-loved, cheerful Dobrai in such condition, and I asked the nurse what was the matter? She told me what I had immediately guessed, that a rumour had spread as to our departure and that the patients were much distressed. Dobrai, who had been taking in and understanding every word she said, turned his big tearful eyes on me. "You're going away—you're going to leave us," he sobbed, as I went up to him and took his hand.

"Ah, yes," I answered, "but even if we do go away, you needn't be unhappy, for you will be sent to a hospital where you will be quite as well cared for as you have been here. In fact," I added, "it's a bigger and a better hospital."

But Dobrai nodded, in the negative: "No no," he sobbed, "where we shall go, we shall be looked after by *fathers*,—but *you* are *mothers*, and that is *much* better."

How I wished that the B.R.C. authorities could have heard those simple words. They have now heard the story, but their only comment has been: "If we had the decision to make all over again, we should make the same decision. We considered the Balkans was not a fit place for white women."

Is it not from decisions such as these, made over the heads of women, against the wishes of women, concerning the work of women—by men who have not taken the trouble even to inquire into the conditions of the work, that rebellious women are created?

But now the fact of our speedy departure soon circulated in the wards, and our patients requested our clever interpreter Adriana to try to express in writing their feelings of gratitude for the work we had been privileged to do for them. The following verses, which ingeniously and naively interpret the sentiments of our Bulgarian soldier-patients, for whom we on our part felt a strong affection, were the result—

A TRUE STORY

Sick and wounded we first came,
Some near death's bridge and some lame,
Far from dear ones, far from home,
Cold, unfed here, there to roam.
But thanks to God, that was not long,
We have to sing thanksgiving song,—
A group of ladies well-prepared
Resolved war-sighs with us to share;
They started from a far-off land,
We think by God they were all sent.
Of cold and mud they never thought,
By working hard our life they bought;
A sweet home they arranged at once,
To see our own they gave us chance.
As pets we were in sister's hand,
With joy their cause we will defend;
So kind and true they all have been
We thought our dear ones we have seen,
And now they gone we'll not forget,
As rose the sun when it has set.
We wish to thank, but find no word,
But God has seen, and knows, has heard.
He may give you double share
For your kind sisterly care;
This is but a simple wish,
Served on plain soldiers' dish.

These verses, which were, it must be remembered, written by a Bulgarian girl, in a language not her own, were signed by a number of the patients themselves, and will ever be to me a precious little document.

The last few days in the hospital were, as can be imagined, full of activity. Stores and equipment had to be checked and packed,—some for return home, some to be given to Dr. Kiranoff, and some to Dr. Moloff, the President of the Bulgarian Red Cross Society, who had throughout been, like everybody else, extremely kind to us. Requisitioned goods had to be sorted and returned to their respective owners. Lists had to be made of men who were well enough to be sent back to their regiments, and of convalescents who would be sent home, and of those who were to be transferred in ox-carts to the barracks-hospital.

The morning of that last day will never be forgotten. Many of the patients, as they were carried on stretchers, or helped with crutches to the carts, were in tears; whilst their more fortunate companions who were going home or back to barracks, and also a large crowd of friends, sympathizers and onlookers, were crowded round the doors of the hospital in the narrow street. Amidst a scene of enthusiastic hand-shaking and hand-kissings and singing of the Shumi Maritza, the last good-byes were said, the remainder of our patients had been lifted into the familiar ox-carts and were disappearing round the last corner of our little street—there was one last wave of hands, and of crutches projected from under the wicker hoods, and—the work was over.

We re-entered the empty hospital to perform the last rites of a work which may, it is hoped, have been not unserviceable to the cause of the Bulgarian nation and to the cause of women.

Florence Nightingale showed years ago that women can be of service in hospitals of war, and broke through much masculine red tape in the process.

The Women's Convoy Corps have shown that women can be of use not only in hospitals of war administered by men, they have shown that women can—without depriving men of their privilege of remaining in the fighting line—improvize and administer, on their own, a hospital of war in all its various departments. They did not, it is true, convoy the wounded from field to base hospital, as they were qualified to do. The Bulgarian military authorities kept this work in their own hands, away from foreigners—from men and from women alike But the women of the Convoy Corps convoyed themselves over country which had just been evacuated by the enemy, under conditions of difficulty which are not likely to offer themselves frequently for repetition within the continent of Europe in modern warfare, and testified undoubtedly to the fact that they could as easily have attended *en route* to wounded soldiers. And they endured whatever hardships and privations they may have encountered, both on their seven days' trek and in their subsequent hospital work, without harm to themselves and without a grumble and complaint, from the first day to the last of the expedition. I myself am an old campaigner in Africa and elsewhere, and no praise can therefore possibly be due to *me* for qualities of endurance or for my share in the undertaking. But I feel it is encumbent upon me to refer to this aspect of the experiment as concerns my companions, because it affords the demonstration which was needed, of the fact that women *can* endure stoically and cheerfully and with safety to themselves, hardships and privations which, being incidental to campaigns of war, have been considered only suitable for men. It is to be hoped that in future, whenever it is thought desirable to send abroad from this country, help for the sick and wounded, units of women as well as units of men may be dispatched by the B.R.C.S.

CHAPTER XXIII

Our return journey to Sofia was not without new interest. The railway-line, though not quite free to Adrianople, was, during he armistice, open to Demotika, and the authorities arranged for us to train through Eskibaba to Demotika, and thence be conveyed in automobiles, or failing these in bullock-waggons again, via Karagali to Mustapha Pasha or Karagatch, where the main line via Phillippopolis to Sofia would be joined. The P.M.O. and Dr. Ivanoff, and other kindly officials and friends, came to the station at Kirk-Kilisse to wish us farewell, and after a fourteen hours' train journey we arrived at Demotika at 1 a.m. Sleeping quarters had been arranged for us in this picturesque rock-townlet. But as we were due to leave Demotika, starting from the station in our automobiles, at eight that same morning, we elected to remain in our railway carriages in a siding for the rest of the night.

We procured for breakfast, glasses of tea at

the station buffet, and started in large government automobiles—for ourselves and luggage—at eight o'clock. We reached the half-way house at Semlin at 1.30, and here we rested and ate luncheon by the roadside. We were close to a field hospital, and sat near the pathetic little wayside burial-ground with its newly dug earth mounds, nameless and unmarked, mute testimony to the folly of mankind. Life—the only one of man's possessions which he himself is powerless to create, the only one of his possessions which he wantonly destroys.

Whilst waiting at Semlin—delayed after the other cars had started—I was fortunate enough to discover that we could, by a little deviation from the direct route, visit the first line of the Bulgarian trenches of investiture round Adrianople, and yet be in time for our train that night at Karagatch. This would involve a slight risk of being benighted on the bad roads of these bleak moorlands; but nothing that is worth doing is accomplished without some risk. The order was therefore given to the chauffeur, "The first line of trenches round Adrianople," and he started off as obediently as though he had been told to drive us to the parish church in England on a Sunday.

We drew up as we saw long lines of Bulgarian

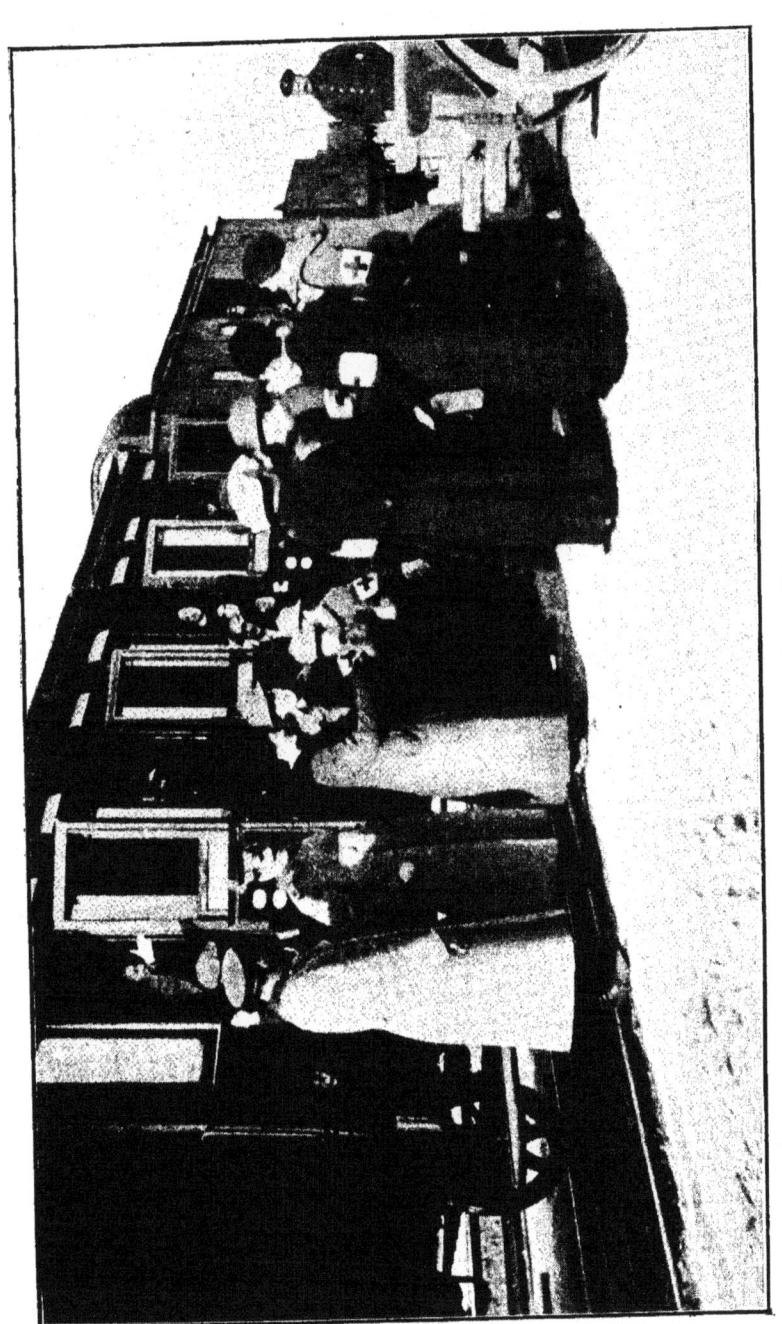

GOOD-BYE TO KIRK-KILISSE.
The P.M.O. on extreme left.

soldiers busy digging and improving trenches which extended along the open country on either side of the road as far as the eye could reach. For though the armistice was in progress, war—as regards preparedness—always continues till peace is declared.

We arrived as the sun was gilding the domes of the four minarets of the beautiful mosque in the besieged city, and the whole town, in the rays of the setting sun, looked so peaceful and fairylike, it was difficult to realize the conditions that prevailed inside the walls. We introduced ourselves to some officers who came to meet us, and they courteously took us round and showed us how they had gradually advanced their trenches, which were visible, line after line in the rear of us, till now, in their present position, they were less than three miles from the promised town.

We were standing on the ridge of an undulating plateau, and upon another ridge, facing us and within a couple of hundred metres, was again a long line of soldiers—differently dressed, who were also busy digging and improving their entrenchments. Between us, and co-extensive with both lines of trenches, was a line of white flags placed at intervals.

"Those white flags," explained our officers,

"betoken during the armistice neutral ground, and those soldiers digging on the other side of the flags are Turkish soldiers in the first line of defence. If war breaks out again, the first shots will be exchanged between them and us," and he pointed to himself. "Would you," asked the officer, "care to have a talk with some of the Turkish officers?" Of course I should. And he accordingly sent a messenger inviting his enemies, whom to-morrow he might shatter into fragments, to come and have a friendly chat!

We watched our messenger till he reached the top of the opposite slope of the hill, and saw him disappear amongst the Turkish soldiers. For some little time there seemed to be no response. Nothing happened. "Perhaps they are refusing to come?" "Oh no," said our officer, "they'll come; we often talk together. But when they hear they are to meet ladies, they will take a long time arranging their toilettes."

In the meantime we were shown the large holes which the Bulgarian soldiers had dug in the ground for night shelters, and I spent a few minutes standing in the trench of this first line of attack, trying to picture, as I aimed with one of the empty rifles at the enemy opposite, what it must feel like to be out to kill one's fellow human beings. No doubt I should, like everyone else, soon get inured, but I felt that henceforth those of us who are *not* condemned to this inurement should at all costs make their protest.

All around us, on both sides of the road, and in the road itself, enormous holes had been excavated by the shells of the defending guns of Adrianople, and innumerable fragments of these shells, of all sizes, as well as empty cartridge cases, covered the ground. We were kept interested, but the toilettes of our Turkish friends might cost us our train connection at Karagatch, and cause us to be benighted and separated from the rest of the party who would await us at the station. I was therefore relieved when finally, just as it grew dusk, we saw striding towards us down the road, two medium-sized figures, with swords hanging beneath the cover of their long grey cloaks.

We advanced to meet them, and round the white flag of truce on that historic road to Adrianople, those two Turkish officers and our Bulgarian officers and our little party of the Women's Convoy Corps, met and chatted together in friendliest fashion. The Turks knew no language but their own, but one of our Bulgarian officers knew Turkish and also French, and in this latter language he acted as intermediary, interpreting into Turkish the remarks I made in French, and *vice versa* for the remarks of the Turks to me.

I broke the ice by telling the Turkish officers that we had been conducting a hospital for the wounded, and that some of our patients had been Turkish soldiers and that they were excellent fellows. In Red Cross work nationalities were non-existent, and it was chance only that had directed us to nurse chiefly Bulgarians. The Turkish officers responded in appreciative terms, but were obviously weary of the war and looked starved and careworn. They wrote their names in Turkish characters —they knew no other—in my note-book, and we all, Turks, Bulgarians and English, talked and even laughed together unrestrainedly.

We bade them good-bye, and as I drove off, and watched the two sets of pretended enemies return each to their respective trenches, the artificiality of war was borne in upon me. These men had no grudge or personal animosity against each other: on the contrary, they met every day on friendly terms. But because the governors of their respective countries are such thickheads—so dull of wit or lacking in

FIELD HOSPITAL NEAR ADRIANOPLE.

imagination that they can devise no better way of securing justice, these peasant fathers of families are told to dig trenches and play bo-peep till a given signal, when they are to dash out and blow each other's brains out. The most successful brain-blowers will then be reckoned to have had justice on their side, and the world will accept the decision with applause. The carnage is given an appearance of seemliness by stage management—according to rules. Murder is not murder when it is done in line and in obedience to military bugle calls! Heavens! How the devil must needs laugh to see his dupes madly rushing to their work of destruction, inspired even to heroic bravery by the specious arguments with which *he* has filled their heads. From his "trial by water" and "trial by fire" we have already escaped; when will his "trial by battle" also be regarded as an anachronism for twentieth-century mankind, and be proscribed and remembered only as a tradition of primeval times when the devil, flaunting his naked tail and hoofs, was allowed to walk unchidden in our midst?

War unfortunately did break out again, and some, if not all, of those men with whom we joked and talked are now, presumably, their jokes all stilled, under the sods in those very trenches. Fools that men are! With each life that is born, the world gains new brains to help in discovering the mystery of life and of the hereafter. But man in his barbarism cries: "No mysteries for me! *Death* is the only thing *I* can understand. I will destroy these brains—I will kill and be satisfied." A large military and journalistic claque, in possession of the big drums and the speaking trumpets, then applauds, and the rest of us feebly clap our hands in acquiescence Until I went to the Balkans I had clapped with the majority. I had of course never doubted that war is an evil, but I had doubted whether there might not be other evils perhaps of a more insidious nature. Might it not perhaps be true, as asserted by the militarists, that "war brings out qualities of heroism and self-sacrifice which would otherwise lie dormant"?—that "the virility of a nation is dependent upon the fighting qualities of its manhood"? I know now that these are devil's arguments. I know now that war kindles, not qualities of heroism, but qualities of *brutality* which would otherwise lie dormant—atrophied with the dorsal appendage, in embryo; that war stifles, suppresses, massacres, qualities of essential value for the future of mankind. It is true that the virility

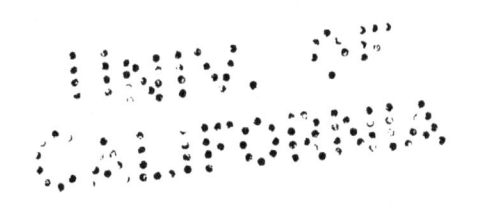

IN THE TRENCHES NEAR ADRIANOPLE.

of a nation *is* dependent on the fighting qualities of its manhood, but the fight which man must wage is not against *Man*, but against the *environment* of Man. *That* distinguishes Man in essence from the brute. Progress in the world of consciousness is one long fight against *environment*—one long battle against that *adaptation to environment* which was the leading-string of pre-human life.

I could not succumb to the environment of war. All day long in our hospital at Kirk-Kilisse, surrounded on the one hand by the butchered bullocks in the kitchen, and on the other by the butchered human beings in the wards, the thought was borne in upon me, Are we then *solely* animals? Are bloodshed and butchered bodies the only things that count? Is there in the world no spiritual element? Is the religion of Christianity only an aspiration? Are the Idealist philosophies of Bergson, Eucken and of those of us who believe in a spiritual future for mankind—only an intellectual bubble? *Does* man truly believe that his evolution is to be along spiritual lines? How then, is it possible for him to assert that the only means to the progress of nations is by the butchery of the bodies of his bravest men and the starvation of his women and children? Is it not time that the world made up its mind as to whether it does or does not believe in this spiritual evolution? Time that it should boldly face those two small words *yes* or *no*—there is no third—and act straightway in accordance with a decision. For those of us who *have* come to a decision, and who believe that the development of mankind will be, not upon the physical or the intellectual, but upon the *spiritual* plane, our duty lies clear. We must acknowledge that war is an unmitigated evil. We must denounce the bestial horrors and indignities to which it subjects human beings. We must no longer condone War as a tragedy, —we must condemn it as a Crime.

CHAPTER XXIV

Our drive in the dark to Karagatch was an exciting race against time. But we were fortunate enough to have no punctures or breakdowns, and we arrived a few minutes before the departure of the train—a military train with special carriages for our party—for Phillippopolis and Sofia. We arrived next evening at Sofia, where the Red Cross authorities, under Dr. Radeff's kind direction, had arranged for our reception at the Hotel de Paris for the night.

The Queen had very graciously expressed her wish to see me again. I proceeded, therefore, the next morning to the Palace. My former impressions of Queen Eleonora were strengthened, and I came to the conclusion that the Bulgarian people had been very fortunate, not only in their choice of King, for his intellectual qualities are well known in Europe, but in the possession of a Queen who combines in a wonderful way a capacity for hard work and mastery of detail, with qualities of intuition, sympathy, and understanding. Her Majesty spoke with much warmth and gratitude of the services rendered to her Bulgarian soldiers by the Convoy Corps. She had, she said, received many reports, official and unofficial, of the progress of our work in hospital, and all alike had been in flattering terms. I confided to her my hesitation as to the right moment for closing the hospital, and Her Majesty replied, "You have chosen exactly the right psychological moment," and, after some personal encomiums which were particularly undeserved, the Queen asked me to accept a photograph of herself framed in silver, and to deliver to each member of the Corps then present with me, a gift which she kindly sent to the hotel.

Dr. Radeff was, as usual, kindly solicitous for our welfare. He must have been overburdened with work and worries, but he never fussed, and that evening, as he accompanied us to the station, helped us with our luggage and saw us into our special carriages, he, with his fine Bulgarian courtesy, conveyed the impression that for the moment his only concern in life was for our well-being.

Our heavy baggage, which had been taken

in charge by the station-master earlier in the day, and placed in a van of its own, had disappeared, together with the station-master. A new station-master for the night-shift knew nothing of our vanload. "It will be sent after you," he said calmly. I begged to differ. There were literally thousands of vans and trucks crowding nearly a mile of lines, and there was small chance of our truck of luggage and equipment extricating itself all on its own. We hunted for the van till it was time for the train to start, then I visited the station-master again. "We are going," I said quietly, "to remain here till you find our luggage. We cannot go back to the hotel again. Please, therefore, give us some railway carriages in which we can spend the night, put us on a siding, then search for our van. We'll depart and leave you in peace when you have found it."

This produced a marvellous effect. We spent the night in unwarmed carriages on a siding, and early in the morning, before it was light, I was aroused from a semi-unconscious condition by hearing something that sounded like an express train coming along our line. The word "collision" was on my lips when a collision occurred,—crash—bang—I was hit on the head by my Gladstone bag, kodak, and other articles which had been hurled from the rack above and ricochetted from my head into the passage outside. I dashed out to see if any of the others in the other carriages were hurt, but found no harm done, only a general scattering of the handbags. I felt very angry with the station-master, and I made for his office, for I had warned him against putting us on a siding which was not safe.

"Madam," he replied quietly, "it was your luggage—anxious to rejoin you. The engine-driver lost control—I am sorry; he will be reprimanded. But now you can leave at seven o'clock."

It was with feelings both of regret and satisfaction that we bade farewell to Sofia and Bulgaria, and started on our return journey via Belgrade, Buda-Pesth, Vienna, Frankfort, Brussels, Calais and Dover, to London. An accident to the Orient Express, of which a portion was smashed to splinters on the main line outside Belgrade, caused some delay, but in due course the Women's Convoy Corps arrived safely back in London, having proved by "practical demonstration" that women *can* be of independent service in time of war? This "practical demonstration" will, it is hoped, in a humble way, help to convince our old friend Public Opinion that it *is* expedient to employ women in warfare, and that the question with which we started this book, "Ought women to take a practical share in National Defence, and to be included as an integral portion of the Territorial army?" may safely be answered in the affirmative.

CHAPTER XXV

BUT even though it may, by the foregoing pages, have been shown that women are capable of taking a share, a serviceable share, in warfare, without inexpediency to any concerned, and even with direct benefit to all concerned, there remain questions of *sentiment* which must not be ignored if we are thoroughly to satisfy our old-fashioned friend Public Opinion.

For we all, as Mill puts it, "have sentiments, but with some people these are adapted to *past* ages, with others to *coming* ages." And those whose sentiments are adapted to the past rather than the future will be feeling discomfort about many points. Why, they may ask, is it necessary that women should come out from their homes to do work like this *at all*? Even granting, if you like, that they *can* do it, and do it well, isn't there plenty of good work to be done *within their own* homes? "A woman's sphere is the home."

But it must be remembered, in answer to

this, that the conditions of home-life have, since the days of our grandmothers, been revolutionized for women by machinery and factories. These accessaries of civilization have deprived women of the natural outlet for activities of an industrial and domestic, as well as of an intellectual, order within the home. In the days when such proverbs as " The woman, the cat and the chimney should never leave the house," "*Bonne femme est oiseau de cage*," "A wife and a broken leg are best left at home," were current in every household, there was some reason why women should remain at home. For *within the home* were conducted—by women—all the industries of life. In those days women not only made jams and pickles, cured the hams and bacon, concocted wines and medicines; they also designed and embroidered all the curtains, tapestries and carpets; the making of beautiful laces, the spinning, the weaving, the sewing and the knitting of all the garments was committed to the charge of women. In those days, when the control of all that made life worth living was with woman, she did not need, nor did she seek, outside occupations, which indeed consisted chiefly of the less intellectual pursuits of hunting and fighting. There was plenty of scope *within* doors for the intellectual, industrious and artistic faculties of every active-minded woman. If it were true that Woman was more honoured at that time, when she remained within the confines of the domestic hearth, than she is now, this was not *because* she remained at home, but because all the arts and crafts of life were in her hands—*within the home.* But now all this is changed, through no fault of the woman herself, and, except for the young wife and mother, who has plenty of occupation in the rearing of her family, there is not enough work *within the home* for additional active-minded and able-bodied women, the unmarried daughters, sisters, cousins, aunts, who need occupation, but who can have no family of their own because there are not enough men to go round.

The care and cleanliness of the home itself is now in a large measure confided to machinery, —and automatic cleaners take the place even of the good old annual spring cleaning which gave holiday to husbands and opportunities to housewives. The result is that, with the best will in the world, women who are not wives and mothers, and who do not need to earn a living, are reduced to finding occupations in futile social functions, bridge parties, motor-driving and flirtations. The more energy and activity a woman possesses, the more energy and activity will she put into these pastimes; and the more seriously she treats these pursuits, the worse it is for herself and for the State.

Duty varies with times and circumstances. It was recorded as a eulogy of the father of Frederick the Great that when he met a woman in the street he would walk up to her with his cane raised, saying, "Go back into the house; an honest woman should keep indoors."

When the work of woman was within the home it was obviously the duty of women to be chiefly within doors. But now that almost every form of possible work for women has been transferred to regions *outside* the domain of home, it becomes just as much the duty of a woman to go outside, and a dereliction of duty to remain within, as it was formerly her duty to remain within, and a dereliction of duty to be frivolous outside.

In the human, as in the animal world, change of environment necessitates change of habit, and change of habit involves again change of character. For women, the whole environment and conditions of life have changed, and, deprived of her ancient sphere of activity *within* the sheltered walls of her own household, woman must now choose between two alternatives.

She must, on the one hand, either content herself with tatting, dusting china ornaments, nursing poodle dogs, and giving herself over to a life of fatuous and supersensual emotions—degenerate, that is, into a social parasite, sucking the very life-blood of the State, or she must seek work in the outer world. The example of the kiwi bird should be a wholesome warning to those women who hanker after the first alternative. This bird, whose natural firmament was celestial space, succumbed to the temptation of following a line which was temporarily one of least resistance, and because food was at one time plentiful *on the ground*, and exacted less exertion in attainment, adapted itself structurally and with apparent temporary advantage to become a *ground bird*. But there came a time when firearms were introduced into New Zealand, and that poor foolish kiwi bird, with its wings now irretrievably atrophied, is likely soon to become extinct. And women, if they do not face the present situation courageously, are liable to suffer, not extinction but degeneration—to lose their wings of independence and become parasites, depending for the means of livelihood upon the efforts, physical and mental, of the other sex. Decadence of all the finer qualities of womanhood must result, if women are to be condemned to a life in which love and intrigue, games, pleasures and social functions are the dominant features. And nothing is more certain than this: if woman degenerates, man's degeneration is not far distant. "Bodies of different weights fall with the same velocity."

Bergson's formula, which he applied to science, applies, it seems, with equal appropriateness to the position of woman to-day. "It is," Bergson says, "an immutable law of the universe, that species pass through alternate periods of stability and transformation. When the period of mutability occurs, unexpected forms spring forth in a great number of different directions." And might we not expect, as a possible contingency, that undue suppression of those new forms will result in the production of monstrosities.

But if woman is to work in the outer world in competition with man, who has indeed already annexed most of her former occupations, if, that is, she is to participate with man on equal terms, in the general work of life, in the rewards of business, art, trades and the professions, and in the benefits of social security and good government, she must share with man the responsibility of *defending* those walks of life and that government, from enemies without, as well as from enemies within.

The modern woman has an instinct that there is a large sphere of work open to her in the Territorial service of her country, when once the sea of prejudice has been safely crossed. Is she, in indulging this instinct, more irrational than say, Columbus, who set sail upon an instinct that the Atlantic had a shore upon the other side?

It is difficult to realize that only fourteen hundred years ago—in the sixth century A.D., a council of the wisest men of the day sat solemnly at Macon to discuss the question as to whether or no women possessed souls and were human beings like unto men, or whether they were indeed merely animals? By a stroke of good luck for us women, the question was eventually decided, though only by a small majority, in the affirmative. Only by the skin of our teeth were we recognized by the world as belonging to humanity! Now, one of two things. Either women must, during the intervening period—between that council of Macon and the time of our grandmothers, the time of man's ideal woman—have made a most miraculous progress, or those men of Macon were wrong in their estimate of the nature of women. In the former alternative is it not possible that, without men's having noticed it, women have gone on progressing, out of recognition—from our grandmothers' times to this year of grace 1913? In the *latter* alternative, if the men of the Macon age were so completely out in their estimates of the nature and capacity of women, as even to doubt their kinship in humanity with men, may not twentieth-century men have perhaps also a little mis-focused the attributes of Woman?

It must also be remembered, by those who use the "sphere of home" argument against the participation of women in national defence, and work outside the home, that twentieth-century methods of quick transit and communication have enlarged for women as well as for men the narrower significance of the word "Home." Though the "home" is still, as it probably always will be, the centre of a woman's life, the word "home" has now for women an imperial and world-wide import, and embraces not merely the few square roods surrounding her home demesne, but the colonial dominions in which her sons and daughters live. A woman's horizon is no longer bounded by her own back-parlour and the parish-hall, but by

Atlantic and Pacific oceans which belong to the human family.

Machinery deprived woman of her ancient sphere of work within the home; but machinery, in the shape of quick means of transit and communication, has now, in reparation, opened for woman the portals of the world. The result is an extension of woman's sense of responsibility to national and even international concerns. Woman now sees that there are national as well as domestic virtues, and that it is no more desirable in the interests of women that men should have a monopoly of *national* virtue, than it is desirable in the interests of men that women should have a monopoly of *domestic* virtue.

But what about the interests of *men*, it may be asked? Is the whole world in future to be conducted in the interests of women only? All the best instincts of *man* revolt against the idea that "his womankind" should be exposed to the cruder realities of war. "The woman who can face bloodshed and atrocities, and endure hardships without wincing, is no longer the woman of man's ideal. The charm of womanhood, with its delicacy of sentiment and feeling, will vanish, and the ideal relationship— a relationship of contrast—between the sexes will be destroyed. Like does not mate with like. Besides, women will no longer want to marry. The dull routine of home-life will stand no chance as against the more adventurous possibilities of a life given to the national service."

But in the first place, it must be borne in mind that the strength of character of a nation is in direct ratio to their struggle against nature's obstacles. Is this truth only applicable to the manhood of the nation? May it not also apply to women, who, so long as they are sheltered and cosseted, cannot develop the finer and more heroic characteristics. Men dislike the hardening process for women, but the moral fibre of women, and therefore eventually of the nation itself is at stake.

As concerns *marriage*, if it should indeed be true that women, who can find practical work in life outside marriage, would no longer be so eager to marry, this would not necessarily be an evil, for it would probably act as an additional incentive to man to *desire* marriage. Marriage has been regarded for women as a profession, in which failure involves, as in other professions, humiliation. Women are trained therefore, under the present régime, to employ all the arts at their disposal to ensure success in their profession. The greater the number of competing women and the more jaded the inclination of men, who are fewer in numbers and can thus pick and choose, the more need is there for arts and wiles and sensuous display on the part of women.

If women were absorbed in professions and occupations, such as farming, architecture, territorial service and the like, and only desired marriage when and because they *loved*, the loss, in the woman, of the wiles and artificialities which formerly stimulated the man to marriage, would be counterbalanced by a more healthy emulation on the part of the man, who would be desirous to obtain something of value which was difficult to get.

Furthermore, it is not as a rule the active and industrious women who shirk motherhood, but the idle women who concentrate on the pleasure derivable from emotions which were intended by nature only as a means towards an end. The history of so-called civilization shows that this end—the ultimate object of love-making between the sexes—is ignored, generally speaking, in proportion to the glorification that is given to the means. If, therefore, the attention of women should be distracted from the preoccupations of sexual allurements, the result would probably be shown, not in a diminishing birth-rate, but in a reduction of white slaves amongst women, and of sensuous pleasure-seekers amongst men.

"Ah!" but it will be again contended, "man's instinctive sense of chivalry requires that woman shall not *defend*; it is she who must be defended. It is the weakness and dependence of woman which brings out all the noblest characteristics of man."

This argument was one day illustrated to me in an interesting fashion by an opponent of this sphere of work for women. He was assuring me, as a reason why it was undesirable that *Women* should participate in national defence, that it would be *very bad for the character of Man*.

He spoke as follows· "It is good for men," he said, "that women should retain their feebleness and feminism. I like," he went on naively, "to feel, when I fondle a helpless kitten on my knee, that I *could* take it and bang its head against the wall. I *don't* do so, and therefore the helpless kitten brings out all my best characteristics!"

But if the "best characteristics" of Man can only be developed by the maintenance of the "helpless kitten" attributes of Woman, and the atrophy of her finer and more self-reliant qualities, then the sooner men and women set to work to devise some other standard of "best characteristics," both for men and for women, the better.

There is much confusion prevalent on the subject of the sex-characteristics of women, owing, I have always thought, to general lack of discrimination between those characteristics of a woman which are incidental to her *sex* and should be truly called qualities of *womanhood*, and those characteristics which are only incidental to her environment and should be recognized as characteristics of *femininity*. The *womanly* qualities are those which are essential for the *preservation of the species;* they are concerned with the primary functions of sex itself; they have been evolved; they are of germ-cell origin, and are inheritable in that sex only to which by nature they belong; they are, in short, qualities which have been hall-marked by God for *creative purposes.*

The instincts of mother-love, of self-sacrifice, of usefulness, these are in Woman essential for the fulfilment of the *Idea of the Species*, for without them the race would die. *These* are the inheritable, ingrained *qualities of womanhood.*

The *feminine* characteristics, on the other

hand, have not been evolved by God,—they have been inculcated by mankind for purposes of an artificial social life. Love of dress and display, inanity, helplessness and idleness—these are not ingredients of the *woman's* nature; these are not *instincts*, they are *habits*, superficial and eliminable. Femininity, exhibited in hobble skirts, corsets, preposterous headgear and high-heeled shoes, is like the blueness of the Andalusian fowl described by Mendel, it is a quality for which in nature there is no gamete. *Man* has made Woman *feminine* for his purpose; God made her *womanly* for *His*.

The characters of *womanhood* as also of manhood are unchangeable, but if the characteristics of femininity and of masculinity, which are dependent upon circumstance and environment, do *not* change with the changes of circumstance and environment, caricatures of both sexes are the result.

And now that a vast change has been effected by machinery, factories and methods of transit and communication, in the circumstances and environment of woman's life, it is inevitable that a change should also take place in those *outer* characteristics which are, however, the characteristics of *femininity only*.

But, it may again be urged, such high-falutin

philosophy might be good enough for books, but let us be practical. Supposing war breaks out, and the woman is called away from her home on active service. What is to happen to the poor wretched man who, if he were not himself in the army or in the Territorial service, would be left to servants, with the care of the children on his hands and his home-life destroyed. And what would happen to the children if the man and the woman both went off on service? The latter case is immediately answered, for no woman with small, unleavable children would join the Territorials. But as regards the possibility of a man being left by wife, sister, aunt or any other home-making relative, it must be borne in mind that in the case of a *man* similarly called upon to leave his home, his wife and his family, the world thinks it very right that he should, in times of national emergency, consider the welfare of the nation before the welfare of his family. This is a higher morality which is not generally disputed. Why, then, should the same high morality not apply equally in the case of woman?

But, it will be argued, men do not desire that women should make these sacrifices. Men are *themselves* willing to make any sacrifice that is required, but it is their privilege to shield "their womenfolk" from such necessity. We all know, they say, that a woman will sacrifice herself for her *home*, her *husband* and her *child*, and that is all we demand of her. We do not desire or deem it fitting that she should sacrifice her home, her husband and her child for her country. That supreme sacrifice is the duty and privilege of man.

But if it is the *sacrifice* which, for the man, constitutes the virtue and the heroism, why should not the greater sacrifice entailed upon the woman, who should leave home and family for work in hospitals of war, constitute, for the woman, an even greater virtue and heroism? Are women to be denied all exercise in the higher and heroic virtues?

If it is important for the character of the male population that they should be ready to make sacrifices for their country, it is difficult to see how it could be bad for the character of woman to make a similar sacrifice? It is true that a discrimination between *national* and *domestic* virtue may be involved, but, as illustrated by those who volunteered for the Boer War, discriminations between patriotic and business claims, patriotic and family claims, were made by men who volunteered their services, and on the whole these discriminations were safely left to the discretion of business men and fathers of families. Is there any reason to suppose that a woman would more likely reject the claims of family and of home duty than a man?

If, then, it be right, according to a higher morality, for women as well as men to make sacrifices — of others than themselves — in national causes, it cannot be less right for them to do so because there may be *accompanying risk*. Women in these days feel that it is no longer desirable for men to decide, either whether women shall take risks, or what the nature of the risk shall be. Women are no longer in their nonage. They are responsible human beings, and are capable of judging for themselves. So long as men kept women from a knowledge of life and of its dangers, so long was it incumbent on men to keep them also from the accompanying and unknown risks. But from the moment that an adult woman understands the risks she may be running, it is for her to determine whether she will take them.

It will probably be argued in reply that risk of *life* which men and women both share in common is one thing, but there are other risks, due to a woman's sex, which she would in warfare have to face, and that it is from *these* risks that men would at all costs protect her. But the sex of woman runs more risks every night in the civilized streets near Piccadilly, under conditions of *civil* law, than is ever likely to be encountered by them under *martial* law. There is no danger so great for women as ignorance. There is no danger in the outside world, or on battlefields, which can compare with the danger incurred through the ignorance of the woman who never leaves "the sphere of home."

And again, if the sacrifice which the woman makes in leaving her home should involve on the *man* the sacrifice of losing her, the deplorable circumstance will be, not the act of sacrifice, but the war which makes such sacrifices necessary. If disaster to the home should come to be for the man, as it has always been for the woman, a corollary of war—an additional incentive towards peace might thus be provided, and women's entrance into the area of war become on this score alone justified?

But again, it may be urged that the welfare of the state depends upon the welfare of the family, which must at all costs be guarded, and that the presence of the woman in the home is essential to the welfare of the family. But existing laws point to the prevalence of the impression that the husband and father is of more value to the family than the wife and mother, and, as concerns the *material* welfare of the home, the result is, under present conditions, probably more disastrous if the man is killed than if the woman dies. For whereas the death upon the battlefield of the man—the breadwinner—may entail the destitution of the family, the death of the wife and mother in a fever hospital would cause to the family at home chiefly sorrow and inconvenience. In any case, it is left to a man's own conscience to decide between his country and his family, and a similar decision could probably be left with equal safety to the conscience of women, to whom the horrors of war would offer less temptation from the path of home-duty than to the man. It is in any case as important for the character of women that they should be *free* to *choose* the form of sacrifice required by the emergency, as it is for men, and there is no reason to suppose that, given the choice, the woman's sense of duty to the home would be less acute than that of her male partner.

There must, at any rate, be no half-measures. The woman who derives benefits from the country must be prepared—*where circumstances permit*—to serve that country in national emergency, and if she engages herself to serve that country she must be ready to make every sacrifice, even the sacrifice of her own feelings, if the emergency arises. And the man who does not want to see the British race die of inanition must sacrifice *his* feelings, and help the women in their new-born desire to *grow a national backbone.*

It is to the interests of men, as members of a dominant race, that the heroic as well as the gentler virtues should be cultivated amongst women. To judge from the numbers of the Territorial army to-day, there is not a glut of self-sacrificing qualities amongst men. The development of a national virtue amongst women might be the salvation of the men, and an incentive to a patriotism in which men and women would vie with each other in wholesome rivalry. And who knows if, when the time should come that men and women should be out together for heroic purposes, it might not come to pass that "the manhood that has been in war will be transferred to the cause of Peace," and war will then, as Emerson predicted, "lose its charm and peace be venerable to men."

CHAPTER XXVI

But now that the War Office has organized, through the B.R.C.S., a system of Voluntary Aid Detachments, in which women are invited to serve, and that this scheme has been, all over the country, largely taken up by women, isn't that enough, it may be asked? But I answer emphatically, *No*. This V.A.D. scheme is, to my mind, worse than nothing. For it acts as a placebo—a bread pill, to dupe women into the belief that they are being treated seriously by the War Office If women are to do *real* Territoral work, they must be made a *real living portion* of the Territorial army. They must work with and under the organization of the Territorial army, and not primarily, as now, under the jurisdiction of a Red Cross Society, which is intrinsically an organization for other purposes. The duplication of authority is crippling in time of peace; it would be fatal in time of war. Conditions of training must, if they are to be of any practical use, be *military* conditions, dictated by *military* authorities. Women who are to perform *national* work should be enlisted and paid as men are paid in the Territorial army, and *real* work, not play work, must be exacted by those who understand the kind of work which would be required in military eventualities.

It is true that at the moment the War Office sends a representative to inspect V.A.D.'s. But these representatives pass their verdict according to standards which are hopelessly inadequate, and inappropriate to real conditions of warfare. The whole thing is a farce—a mere drawing-room game, conducted upon the principle that women are incapable of anything but amateur nursing. More and more stress is laid upon the importance of the "linen frock and white apron" hospital work, on the assumption that the only place for volunteer women in warfare will be within hospital wards.

But from experience of what I saw and heard in the Balkan hospitals—other than our own—it is precisely within the wards of hospitals that volunteer and amateur women who are *untrained and undisciplined* are least wanted. *Within the wards* trained nurses who have been subjected to discipline, not the least valuable portion of their training, and who have given up their lives to the work, are for many reasons essential. Volunteer women are wanted to render *first-aid* in every department of work that occurs between the removal of the wounded from the field-hospital, to their arrival at the base hospital. They should certainly be able to render first-aid in nursing, as in bandaging, convoy work, cooking and all the branches of work within the area specified, but should *not* be allowed to regard themselves as *trained nurses.* The result in the wards in time of war would be deplorable.

Women who are to be *efficient* in the Territorial sphere must be given opportunities of training and discipline similiar to those which are given to Territorial R.A.M.C. men. The triviality of the training, the lack of discipline and the haphazardness of the whole V.A.D. scheme, as now in practice, would result in fiasco in time of emergency, and the whole cause of women's work in national service would be seriously prejudiced.

It is true that a severer and more military régime would probably exclude thousands of women who now proudly rejoice at having obtained medals for attending half a dozen lectures on first-aid and home nursing. But this elimination is essential to serious work. There are at the moment thousands of women on the V.A.D. registers who would be a grave hindrance to real work in time of emergency. As long as they are allowed to play around in the movement, so long will the movement be a mockery of the aspirations of earnest and capable women. It would be far better for the nation to have at command a few *hundred* trained and disciplined women upon whom in emergency reliance could be placed, than to permit hordes of undisciplined women to be registered as members of V.A.D.'s and to regard themselves as fully qualified, without discrimination as to capacity and training, to take positions of responsibility in time of war.

I plead that women who are seriously desirous of joining the Territorial army *as workers* should be allowed to form a supplementary Army Medical Corps of women, to act in conjunction with the R.A.M.C. of men, and to be subject to the same authority as the men.

Is it not a suggestive thought for those who still doubt the capacity of women to do this, that, or the other thing which has hitherto been done only by men, that throughout the whole range of chemistry *similarity of arrangement means similarity of property*. The properties of the atoms are dependent on the *arrangement* of the corpuscles of which they are composed. It is not the intrinsic quality, or size, or weight of the atom, but *arrangement* which gives character. Whatever may be the difference in the comparative weights of respective atoms, there will be similarity of property if there is similarity of arrangement in the corpuscles of which they are composed. Is it unreasonable to assume that the differences between the characters of men and of women respectively, is due chiefly to the differences of *arrangement*, or of training, which they undergo?

There is little, if any, of the work which is at present being performed by the men of the R.A.M.C. which could not be done by women, and even though the authorities should still wish to prevent women from coming on to the actual field of battle, there is plenty of other R.A.M.C. work which could still be accomplished by women.

So long as there is a shortage in Territorial numbers, it is wasteful to draw off able-bodied men from the fighting line to do any work which could be done by women.

The summation, however, of the whole argument is this. The changed conditions of woman's life have forced her from the narrow circle of her own home to the broader arena of the outside world. Here she has to compete for a livelihood with man, in the business, arts, trades, and professions of life. But it is clear that if woman is to share with man the advantages of a government which protects her industries and means of livelihood, she must share with man in the responsibility of defending that government from foes without as well as from foes within. The question as to whether woman should share in the *government* of her country is a part of the woman question with which we are not here dealing. But it is in any case transparent that the *duty of participating in the defence of a country follows as a corollary to participation in work and benefits provided by that country.*

If, however, woman is to defend the country in a serviceable way, as a *duty* and not a game, she must be seriously trained, not only in the work, but also in the discipline which the proper conduct of the work demands. And if she is to be trained and disciplined and thus made of practical service to the country, she must be rewarded as men are rewarded, by pay, and titles, and ranks, which are recognized in the Territorial army as the rewards for *definitely recognized work.* Her work would then be a national service, and should be under the same control as the national service of men. The energies and activities formerly contributed by women to the work conducted within the home, needs appropriating and channelling if it is not to bring disaster to the community. Could there be a more serviceable aqueduct for the surplus activity of those seriously-minded women who are now at a loose end, than employment in the Territorial service of their country?

It is now hoped that the *practical demonstration* which the Women's Convoy Corps have given, in the Balkans, of the capacity of women to be of independent service and to endure practical difficulties in the sphere of war, without hindrance to others or harm to themselves, may help, if only in a humble way, to convince our old friend Public Opinion of the *expediency* of answering in the affirmative the question with which we started this book · "Ought women to take a practical share in National Defence, and to be included as an integral portion of the Territorial Service?"

"He who wishes to cling to the old that ages not must leave behind him the old that ages." May I then, in conclusion, ask those who base their opposition to woman's participation in the more active work of the outer world, and who still cling to their time-worn fetish "a woman's sphere is the home," to remember that the women who desire to serve their country are not, as a rule, the women who neglect—they are, on the contrary, the women who would *defend* their homes. They have no desire to relinquish their old ideal of being the "guardian angels" of the home. But they now regard "home" in the larger sense of *Country* and of *Empire*, and desire to be allowed to share with Man the larger morality of the larger term.

If the men who are in authority at the War Office, and elsewhere, would learn to distinguish between *women* and *femininities*, they would not be afraid as to the result of this new desire on the part of women. They would then understand the significance of the old Friulean saying, "What the Woman wanteth, God wanteth; and what God wanteth, cometh to pass."

THE END

Printed by MORRISON & GIBB LIMITED, *Edinburgh*.

Crown 8vo.   2s. 6d. net

The Future
of the
Women's Movement

By Mrs. H. M. SWANWICK

WITH AN INTRODUCTION BY

Mrs. H. FAWCETT

Mrs. Swanwick writes as a strong believer in the Women's Movement, but as an opponent of militancy. She reviews every phase of the present position of women, with special emphasis on its economic aspects, and a feature of her book is her firm, unhesitating treatment of the problem of commercialized vice.

SOME OF THE TOPICS DISCUSSED.

Causes of the Women's Movement—What is the Women's Movement?—The Subjection of Women—Physical Force—Democracy and Representative Government — Votes — The Economic Problem: (i) The Wage Earner; (ii) The Mother; (iii) The Housewife; (iv) The Prostitute; (v) Commercialized Vice—The Man's Woman—The Woman's Woman—Sex Antagonism—The Old Adam and the New.

LONDON: G. BELL AND SONS LTD.
YORK HOUSE, PORTUGAL STREET, W.C.

THIS BOOK IS DUE ON THE LAST DATE STAMPED BELOW

AN INITIAL FINE OF 25 CENTS
WILL BE ASSESSED FOR FAILURE TO RETURN THIS BOOK ON THE DATE DUE. THE PENALTY WILL INCREASE TO 50 CENTS ON THE FOURTH DAY AND TO $1.00 ON THE SEVENTH DAY OVERDUE.

NOV 5 1933

NOV 6 1933

NOV 7 1933

Oct '58 HK

NOV 17 1958 L U

APR 3 1972

DEC

AUG 04 1998

295415

Stobart
DR46
S8

UNIVERSITY OF CALIFORNIA LIBRARY